Teaching social studies
for critical, active citizenship
in Aotearoa New Zealand

Teaching social studies for critical, active citizenship in Aotearoa New Zealand

Edited by Michael Harcourt,
Andrea Milligan and Bronwyn Wood

NZCER PRESS

NZCER PRESS
New Zealand Council for Educational Research
PO Box 3237
Wellington
New Zealand

www.nzcer.org.nz

ISBN 978-0-947509-41-5

A catalogue record for this book is available from the National Library
of New Zealand

Designed by Smartwork Creative Ltd

Contents

Foreword

It is a great honor to write a foreword to this volume. By way of introduction, I am one of a handful of US social studies teacher educators who have had the great fortune to work and live in New Zealand. In 2013, I spent 8 months at Victoria University of Wellington as a Fulbright Scholar, and was hosted by Mark Sheehan, a senior lecturer at VUW. While at VUW, I met Andrea, Bronwyn and Michael, part of the talented group of social studies educators currently working at the institution. Since then, Michael and I have collaborated with Mark on a research project on Māori and Pākehā adolescents' views of the Treaty of Waitangi. I've also gotten to know and read the work of Andrea and Bronwyn, and have come away from all of these experiences both smarter and wiser.

I have taught social studies education courses at several different universities within the US over the past 30 years. I also have collaborated on research with colleagues from across the globe. My research examines how young people's ethnic identities influence their understandings of their nation's histories and contemporary societies, as well as how teachers can or do organise instruction to promote young people's understandings of and dispositions towards social justice. It is from these experiences that I am writing these remarks. I don't presume to 'tell' New Zealand social studies educators anything about what they are or should be doing. It may be helpful, however, to make comparisons between the social studies issues raised in these pages and those that resonate (or not) within a US context. My comments then serve as a comparative analysis of the contexts, concepts and practical concerns that surround social studies education in our two societies, and what US educators may learn from New Zealanders.

Social studies education in westernised democratic nations in a global age

Like most in the US, I knew little if anything about New Zealand before I lived there. Now, however, I am struck by the deep similarities between our nations, derivative of our national histories of European conquest and the establishment of western-oriented, democratic, capitalist societies. Many of the challenges that both societies face today are a result of our histories and contemporary circumstances as 'first world' nations in an age of globalisation. Both societies face problems from growing economic and political divides among our populace; increasing immigration from less wealthy or politically repressive nations; and recurring ethnic tensions among citizens who are equal in principle but not practice. In short, many of the same economic, political, social and cultural tensions characterise both societies. The similarities of our broader contexts may explain why many of the issues presented in this book are similar to social studies issues circulating among teachers and teacher educators in the US. Despite the similarities, I am struck by some very significant differences in how social studies education is defined in official and institutional contexts and how these differences drive what we as social studies educators write about and practice.

The multiple meanings of social studies

As the first through fourth chapters of the book make clear, there are and always have been multiple contested meanings about the purpose and nature of social studies education in New Zealand and the US. While all agree that social studies is related to the concept of "citizenship", the meaning of citizenship and preparation for it have varied tremendously across time and place. As the authors of the first four chapters aptly illustrate, social studies education in schools has meant everything from disciplinary based knowledge about government, history and other social science subjects, to an interdisciplinary integration of social science disciplines used to encourage students to understand social issues and their responses to them, to what the editors have called a "maximal" concept of social studies education, one that views knowledge acquisition as a means to enable young people to participate critically and actively in society. It is this focus on critical deliberation of important issues and social action that the volume advocates.

Currently in New Zealand, *The New Zealand Curriculum* (*NZC*) (Ministry of Education, 2007) organizes the social studies curriculum around the goals of conceptual understanding and social inquiry. The first chapter informs us that the *NZC* promotes conceptual understanding of broad concepts such as society, change, conflict, social justice, etc. that cut across disciplinary boundaries. It also highlights social inquiry skills, such as posing a social issue to investigate, gathering information, exploring different perspectives and proposing solutions. Nevertheless, many social studies teachers continue to focus on traditional sets of knowledge and skills, in part because of the multiple meanings that social studies has acquired and because teachers haven't received effective training in using social inquiry skills to promote conceptual understanding.

The second chapter demonstrates another population for whom social studies concepts, and specifically citizenship, has taken on multiple meanings. The complex and contested concept of citizenship for Māori is rooted in their indigeneity and the tension between universal individual rights on the one hand, and indigenous collective rights to self-determination on the other. This fascinating duality illustrates the complexity involved in conceptual understanding in real world contexts and provides an authentic example of social inquiry into the meanings and challenges of Māori and others' citizenship in contemporary society.

The third chapter provides the historical and conceptual backdrop to issues-based social studies education, and illustrates how the approach can provide experiences of "citizenship *in practice* because it presents an entry point for students' own deliberations about critical, active and ethical participation in society". The chapter's insistence on promoting among young people nuanced and multi-perspectival understandings of issues fits well with the fourth chapter's definitions of, distinctions among and use of viewpoints, values and perspectives in social studies teaching. As with each of the chapters, the fourth chapter provides practical suggestions for teaching young people to use the three concepts to build their understanding of their interconnections and of how they operate in the real world.

From a US perspective, what is most surprising about the section as a whole is that despite the fact that many New Zealand teachers still teach traditional social studies knowledge in traditional ways, the national curriculum emphasises conceptual understanding and social inquiry. This is not the case with official curricular frameworks in the US. Most are still concerned with transmitting traditional historical, political and economic knowledge and traditional skills development, such as writing a persuasive essay by using primary or secondary sources. And many states, such as New York where I live, have high-stakes social studies tests, based on knowledge acquisition and essay writing, and are used as gatekeepers for high school graduation. Although US social studies teacher educators write about progressive approaches to teaching social studies and have documented their efforts in working with teaching and students (Rubin, 2012; Epstein, 2014; Hess, 2015), this work often goes against the grain to traditional approaches to teaching and learning.

New directions in social studies research and teaching

While the first four chapters examined in compelling ways foundational concepts and perennial debates, the next four chapters explored newer issues, at least for social studies educators in the US. Chapter 5 included an original design for teaching and learning social studies as social action for social justice. The four-stage cycle of social inquiry was not just thoughtful but 'do-able'. By integrating knowledge acquisition, social action and reflection into the design, the chapter addressed several significant ideas about what is worth knowing, acting and reflecting upon in the context of social studies classrooms. A few studies in the US have examined how teachers have implemented social action projects (Epstein, 2014) or what students learned (or not) from these types of projects (Sonu, 2012), but social action social studies approaches are still on the margins of pedagogical practices in the US.

Like Chapter 5, Chapter 7 introduced a knowledge/skills based concept—multiple literacies—to social studies education. I appreciated the chapter's broad definition of literacies, embedding the concept within a sociocultural framework of what it means to teach, learn and know. While many in the US have written about social studies education within the context of 'diverse cultural contexts' (race/ethnicity; secular/religious; urban/rural, etc.), few if any have examined linguistic diversity (as in the example of Māori language use). And despite the spread of technology in schools, I know of no US studies that have examined how these technologies have or can advance young people's conceptual understanding in social studies.

Chapter 6 discusses the emotional dimensions of teaching and learning in social studies classrooms, a topic that has received little attention in the US and elsewhere. Anyone who has taught social studies knows that some topics are not just politically or socially contested or controversial; topics about injustice produce emotional responses. Unpacking the risks that teachers face or fear facing in dealing with emotionally charged issues and discussing some of the approaches that teachers might take to make emotional encounters less risky is a significant and under-researched topic, and the chapter has contributed to the ground-breaking work of Zvi Bekerman in Israel and Michalinos Zembylas in Cyprus (Bekerman & Zembylas, 2011, 2016).

The final chapter reminds teachers and teacher educators that "for assessment to be effective it needs to make a strong contribution to improving students' learning and teachers' teaching." The chapter's clear explanations and examples of different types of assessments, and especially those related to social inquiry and to the distinction between discrete knowledge and broad concepts, focus on a broader range of knowledge, skills and dispositions than is currently the case of assessment based research in the US, with its emphasis on knowledge acquisition and skills-based learning (Breakstone, 2014). Internationally, more innovative approaches to assessment of historical thinking can be found in Erickan and Seixas (2015).

Opportunities and challenges

This book raises great opportunities and ongoing challenges for social studies education and educators. The many innovative approaches in this book to defining and organising social studies teaching and learning provide guidance for New Zealand teachers and teacher educators to make their classrooms more authentic, challenging and rewarding contexts for learning. As a US educator, I am a bit envious of the freedom, at least in theory, that the *NZC* provides teachers in offering more creative and engaging approaches to learning. New Zealand is not as test-obsessed as many US states, and high-stakes testing continues to narrow what educators teach and students learn. In addition, the chapters' thorough and thoughtful research on and discussions of social inquiry and action; culturally framed purposes and knowledge; issues-based learning; viewpoints, values and perspectives; emotional dimensions of teaching; multiple literacies; and assessment provide refreshing reminders to researchers outside of New Zealand to broaden our views of what's significant and possible.

At the same time, ongoing challenges face social studies teachers and teacher educators throughout the world. Narrow concepts of social studies education, lack of professional development opportunities for teachers, increasing immigration and lack of attention to what "citizenship" education is or ought to be in increasing diverse classrooms, and growing political divisions within societies that make social inquiry or action a risky endeavor continue to challenge social studies educators interested in transforming the status quo. However, the breadth and depth of the ideas explored in this book give me hope for the future; social studies education in New Zealand is in the capable hands of those who have contributed to this book, and social studies educators within and beyond New Zealand can learn much from their visions.

Professor Terrie Epstein
City University of New York

References

Bekerman, Z. & Zembylas, M. (2011). The emotional complexities of teaching conflictual historical narratives: The case of integrated Palestinian–Jewish schools in Israel. *Teachers College Record, 113*(5), 1004–1030.

Bekerman, Z. & Zembylas, M. (2016). Identity negotiations in conflict-ridden societies: Historical and anthropological perspectives. *Paedagogica Historica, 52*(1), 201–218.

Breakstone, J. (2014). Try, try again: The process of designing new history assessments. *Theory and Research in Social Education, 42*(4), 453–485.

Epstein, S. (2014). *Teaching civic literacy projects: Student engagement with social problems.* New York, NY: Teachers College Press.

Erickan, K. and Seixas, P. (2015). *New directions in assessing historical thinking.* New York: Routledge.

Hess, D. E. & McAvoy, P. (2015). *The political classroom: Evidence and ethics in democratic education.* New York, NY: Routledge.

Ministry of Education (2007). *The New Zealand curriculum.* Wellington: Learning Media.

Rubin, B. (2012). *Making citizens: Transforming civic learning for diverse classrooms.* New York, NY: Routledge.

Sonu, D. (2012). Illusions of compliance: Performing the public and hidden transcripts of social justice education in neoliberal times. *Curriculum Inquiry, 42*(2), 240–259.

Introduction

In Aotearoa New Zealand, social studies has been, and remains, the primary vehicle for citizenship education (Archer & Openshaw, 1992; Wood & Milligan, 2016). Within *The New Zealand Curriculum* (*NZC*) (Ministry of Education, 2007), social studies plays a pivotal role as an integrated platform for learning across the social sciences, and is the key learning area in which students can develop the knowledge and skills of critical and active citizenship. Citizenship is an important cross-curricular theme of the *NZC*, as reflected in the document's vision, principles, key competencies, and future focus themes. It is also an aspect of learning areas such as science and health, but most specifically the Social Sciences learning area, where students will "explore how societies work and how they themselves can participate and take action as critical, informed and responsible citizens" (p. 30). This book focusses on social studies as the compulsory learning area for all students in Years 1–10 (ages 5–15), and as an optional senior subject in the senior school (Years 11–13) alongside other social sciences such as geography, history and economics.

Despite the important role of social studies in citizenship education, the subject has not historically been well served with curriculum support or classroom research, and policy priorities other than citizenship education have predominated (Wood, Milligan, & Morgan, 2013; Schultz, Ainley, Fraillon, Kerr, & Losito, 2010). Furthermore, we are increasingly concerned at the subject's marginalisation in primary schools. There is now evidence of almost no increment in learning occurring between Years 4 and 8 (Ministry of Education, 2015), a narrowing of the curriculum related to "curriculum obesity" (Hill, 2005), poor quality social studies learning experiences (Education Review Office, 2006; Ministry of Education, 2015), and a preoccupation with national testing in literacy and numeracy (Thrupp & White, 2013). One exasperated New Zealand teacher educator has remarked that transformative social studies education may be a lofty ideal, but any social studies learning in primary teaching would be a good start! Furthermore, frequently ad hoc, hit and miss, or content-heavy approaches to social studies in secondary schools means that students could easily avoid learning about active, critical citizenship in the lifetime of their school learning.

We support recent calls for citizenship education to occupy a central place in the senior secondary school, in light of emerging signs of young people's disengagement from traditional forms of political expression (Electoral Commission, 2015; Constututional Advisory Panel, 2013). However, we stress that primary and junior secondary social studies education plays a pivotal role in developing young people's citizenry in Aotearoa New Zealand and that there is an urgent need to support social studies educators at all levels of the curriculum to fulfil the goal of creating critical and active citizens.

This edited collection addresses these concerns. Building on previous edited publications for social studies education in Aotearoa New Zealand (Openshaw, 1992; Benson & Openshaw, 1998, 2005; Wood, Milligan & Morgan, 2013), this book presents contemporary research and thought in social studies education that will equip educators to prepare students as citizens in an uncertain, complex, and challenging world. In this endeavour, knowledge alone is not enough. Social studies education must help students to consider the kind of world they want for themselves and others, and how they can bring about social, environmental, and political change. This includes an examination of their own and others' identities, values, and beliefs and the factors that have shaped them. Learning in social studies also empowers students to maintain what they already value about their communities and society. This is why we believe children and young people need a social studies education that focuses on both critical and active forms of citizenship.

This book offers a direct challenge to the idea that social studies education is about preparing students to fit easily and uncritically into existing society. As an alternative, it explores how social studies and citizenship education can support learners to critically navigate and take action in society during their time in our schools and in their futures. Drawing on expertise from numerous researchers and practitioners, the book invites readers to consider current practices in social studies and citizenship education, and the future directions that may better enable children and young people to reshape their social worlds. It directly engages with perennial issues in social studies education and provides discussion, debate, and evidence-based research to support educators as they mediate these issues.

Navigating and taking action in a complex and changing social world

Young people in Aotearoa New Zealand and around the world face a number of unprecedented and complex social challenges. Cogan and Derricott (2000) suggest that some of these include:

> the globalization of the economy, a significant level of deterioration in the quality of the global environment, rapidly changing technologies …, the loss of a sense of community and shared belief in the common good, ethical questions regarding the use of genetic engineering, large-scale migration both within and between nations and rising crime. (p. 1)

Awareness of these perceived challenges has been heightened by the quickening pace of transnational flows of products, information, images, media, values, and people. National and global events—such as growing international migration, the loosening of nation-state borders, threats of terrorism and growing technological and communication capabilities—have challenged traditional assumptions about status, identity and belonging (Heater, 1999; Isin & Turner, 2007; Osler & Starkey, 2005). Such changes have contributed to a growing interest in promoting informed, critical, and active citizenry in an effort to address the scale and complexity of contemporary challenges.

Internationally, citizenship education has emerged in recent years as a key policy platform through which governments hope to equip students with the knowledge, skills, and dispositions to face complex issues and to work out ways to create a world they want for themselves and others. Citizenship education increasingly requires not only knowledge and understanding about society, but also the development of skills and behaviours as part of an active process of participation, or what some refer to as 'active' citizenship education (Nelson & Kerr, 2006; Ross, 2012). Aitken (2005) refers to these two components of citizenship education as civic literacy and civic participation. In this book we take the position that social studies education needs *both* components as part of a young person's learning, and we suspect that most people reading this book would agree. Consider, for example, the actions of students at a New Zealand urban secondary school witnessed by one of the editors—a colourful, passionate and entirely student-conceived, display of concern about racism:

In 2014, shortly after the grand jury's decision not to prosecute a United States police-man for the murder of Michael Brown in Ferguson, Missouri, a number of students took part in a type of art installation protest to highlight the issues of racism. The students used glass paint to cover the school's foyer with slogans such as "don't shoot" and "never forget". Photographs of the police officer's face were taped on to the wall, crossed out and KKK written above them. Photographs of Michael Brown's face were displayed with a halo over the top. Additionally, lists of many African American people shot and killed by police officers were listed on the glass in the school entrance way. While in this school the students didn't get in 'trouble', very little was made of their protest and after a few days the display was removed from the foyer.

This illustration highlights a missed opportunity for gaining civic knowledge and learning about how to participate in a democracy. Social studies teaching and learning that more intentionally brought together civic literacy with civic participation could have significantly supported these students' ability to respond to the issue. Had there been, for example, greater opportunity for students to think beyond two sides to a story (such as 'Black versus White'), and to consider the complexities of racism and the different ways people have responded to it (especially racism in their own country), the actions described above might have flowed from a greater depth of knowledge and reflection. Moreover, these kinds of issues provide openings for young people to consider which types of actions could bring about change, and the role that they can play as current citizens in their democracy, not just citizens-in-waiting.

Such experiences provide an ideal context for young people to take part in authentic, engaged, and critical learning about society. As Meyer (1998) argues that, "because it is contentious, social studies gives us the ideal set of circumstances for developing young people who are critical thinkers and responsible decision-makers" (p. i). However, as the story above illustrates, such experiences all too often can have the exact opposite effect: in many schools young people are reprimanded for acting out, discouraged from further action, or told to 'keep politics out of the playground'. Further, evidence from New Zealand classrooms reveals that social studies learning commonly focuses primarily on knowledge and literacy development, and rarely embraces the contested and controversial nature of social issues (Harrison, 1998;

Keown, 1998; Wood, 2013). This presents a significant dilemma to educators who are charged with delivering the type of citizenship education that will lead to a sustained commitment to active participation in a democracy, when the contexts within which young people operate generally inhibit their actual power to make decisions or enact change. Such hierarchical settings reduce young people's ability to participate as active and critical citizens during their time at school.

In this book, we set out to provide social studies teachers with the ideas, research, and vision to nurture critical and active citizens in their classrooms. Authors in this collected edition embrace the contested and controversial nature of social studies education and have provided rich suggestions for deep learning with the aim of developing autonomous thinkers, and citizens who are able to contribute to a just, democratic, and sustainable society (Gilbert, 2013).

Towards 'maximal' forms of citizenship education in New Zealand

The contested nature of citizenship is most clearly evident in the history of New Zealand social studies education. Citizenship has been central to the curriculum since the landmark *Thomas Report* (Department of Education, 1944), which first formally articulated the integrated subject we still call social studies. This report set out the expectation that students were to perform community service and take an "active place in New Zealand society as a worker, neighbour, homemaker and citizen" (pp. 5, 31). However, the kind of active place expected to be taken by young people conforms more closely to what McLaughlin (1992) has called a *minimal* conception of citizenship. This kind of citizenship emphasises content and knowledge acquisition about a country's history, geography, and system of government, with a central purpose to "inform through the provision and transmission of information" (Kerr, 1999, p. 13). In contrast, *maximal* conceptions of citizenship acknowledge the place of knowledge acquisition but also demand that teachers "use that information to help students to understand and to enhance their capacity to participate" (p. 13).

In the decades following World War Two, social studies curricula sat between minimal and maximal approaches to citizenship (Wood, Taylor, & Atkins, 2013, p. 88). The *Syllabus for Schools: Social Studies in the Primary School* (Department of Education, 1961) expected students to "think clearly about social problems, to act responsibly and intelligently to social situations, and to take intelligent and sympathetic interest in the various peoples, communities, and cultures of the world" (p. 31). Marking a clear change in direction, the 1977 syllabus (Department of Education, 1977) was more radical in its intent and explicitly named social action as a central idea for teachers to consider.

However, this more maximal approach was by no means on steady ground. The 1990s was an era of unusually contested curriculum politics, in which approaches to citizenship were heavily debated (Hunter & Keown, 2001; Mutch, 1998; Openshaw, 1998), with one commentator arguing that the 1994 draft social studies curriculum would "hasten the process of turning out rebellious, bored students who know very little about anything substantive" (Brooke, 1995). The debate largely reflected long-standing issues regarding the purpose of social studies curriculum that included at least two central questions. Should social studies education be a conservative project supporting students to fit into society and replicate their current social class, aspirations and status (that is, for social reproduction)? Or should it be a more radical project requiring students to critique, challenge and transform society (that is, for social reconstruction)? By the time the social studies curriculum development of this period was completed in 1997, social action had been removed as a distinct concept and reduced to the safer 'social decision-making'.

Most recently, the *NZC* (Ministry of Education, 2007) has arguably reasserted the potential for more maximal versions of citizenship education. For example, the concept of social action has been revived within the social studies curriculum, which states that students will "participate and take action as critical, informed, and responsible citizens" (p. 17). While the terms social action and take action remain open to interpretation, there now at least appears to be greater opportunity for forms of citizenship education that enable social studies students to develop deep conceptual understanding about pressing social issues that matter to their lives, and take action informed by what they have learnt.

Social transformation as a primary goal of social studies and citizenship education

Acknowledging multiple hues of citizenship education, this book makes a commitment to maximal and, in particular, critical and transformative approaches. In this book we use the term social transformation to describe societal change that does not privilege Western models (UNESCO, 2014) and to mean an educative orientation that:

- engages social studies learners in recognising, exploring and responding to injustices

- emphasises considered social criticism and informed, iterative social action.

- enfolds young people's understanding of broader social change with their own life-worlds; for example, their emotions, daily practices, relationships, values and consciousness (Gibson, 2009).

A transformative orientation to social studies education connects civic literacy and civic participation and is directed towards social and environmental justice. A central task of this book is to provide research-based understanding and empirical evidence to help social studies educators define and enact transformative social studies education in ways that match the complex social challenges that face young people.

However, there are some very real challenges for a transformative approach, many of which reprise past debates. A key question that a number of authors address in this book, which has been a matter of ongoing deliberation, is *What is the nature of knowledge in social studies education?* Should social studies develop the critical and analytical skills of the social sciences, or emphasise more holistic approaches that recognise cultural knowledges and the need for young people to develop the synthetic skills required to address social issues (Ross, 1985; Ross & Marker, 2005)? The work of Michael Young and others (see Young & Muller, 2010), reflects a growing concern at the emptying out of 'powerful' disciplinary knowledge in education which, they argue, risks excluding already socially disadvantaged learners. While we share the concern about 'over-socialised' knowledge, we contend that social transformation rests on the articulation between disciplinary knowledge and young New Zealanders' cultural and everyday knowledges (Catling & Martin, 2011; Gilbert, 2013). This is because access to multiple ways of being and knowing strengthens our learners' capacity to navigate in their plural and complex communities.

A second challenge reflects the plurality of visions for social transformation, and brings us to the second central question this book addresses: *How do social studies students learn critical and active citizenry?* Just as contentiousness is the stuff of social studies, so will the aims of social studies education be perceived differently by members of the public, teachers and learners. Such differences underpin the contested notions of citizenship and the differing cultural, political and social interpretations of this concept in different contexts (Lister, Smith, Middleton, & Cox, 2003; Nelson & Kerr, 2006; Ross & Marker, 2005). Navigating these differences inevitably presents ethical dilemmas for social studies teachers and their school communitites, and teachers may often unwittingly find themselves negotiating complex territory—as was evident in a very public stoush between a group of Ōtaki primary school students and Michael Laws, then Mayor of Wanganui:

In September 2009 the actions of a class of young Māori students were splashed across the headlines of all major newspapers in New Zealand. These students from Ōtaki School's kura kaupapa (Māori immersion) unit had written letters in te reo (Māori language) to Mayor Laws, urging him to insert and "h" into the city's name. The students' letter argued that Wanganui should be spelt W*h*anganui, which reflected a recent recommendation by the New Zealand Geographic Board and Māori uses of the words 'whanga' (harbour) and 'nui' (big). In his response, the Mayor accused their teacher of putting the students up to the letter-writing, saying that they should not be "angry about something inanimate" (Newton & Francis, 2009.). For Mayor Laws, this was not the kind of participation that the school should be fostering, nor should the matter be of concern to students from another town. His comments illustrate many commonly-held assumptions by adults about what young people should be interested in and how they should participate in society. Such assumptions perpetuate deficit notions of the intelligent, creative, and critical role young people play in society.

Outline of this book

Recognising the previously described challenges, this book supports pre-service and in-service teachers, policy developers, and government and non-government resource providers to consider the critical and transformative potential of citizenship education. The two key questions identified above are tackled in different ways throughout the following chapters, as each author addresses how social studies programmes, practices, and publications can better equip young people to face complex social challenges.

In Chapter 1, Jane Abbiss sets the scene for the book by establishing the knowledge basis for the subject of social studies. She clarifies the integrated nature of the subject in New Zealand and its relationship to the disciplinary traditions of the interpretative social sciences. Perhaps most significantly, Chapter 1 argues that the subject's contribution to disciplinary knowledge derives from its emphasis on understanding the contested nature of social issues.

In Chapter 2, Hēmi Dale discusses how the Māori medium social sciences learning area, Tikanga ā Iwi, connects to broader aspirations of te ao Māori. Placing this learning area within its historical and political context, some of the challenges faced by those developing this marautanga/curriculum are described, especially in regards to the integrated nature of social studies. His chapter outlines how Tikanga ā Iwi is underpinned by Māori values, knowledge and ways of being, central to which are Māori conceptions of active citizenship and indigeneity. Dale describes the emancipatory intent of Tikanga ā Iwi that, in his view, has enabled a greater expression of Māori self-determination.

Chapter 3 outlines the long tradition of issues-based citizenship education, both internationally and in New Zealand social studies curricula. Andrea Milligan, Pip Hunter, and Michael Harcourt establish why a focus on issues is important for social studies and citizenship education, advocate social inquiry as a key methodology through which learners can explore issues, and suggest strategies for encouraging nuanced thinking about such issues.

In Chapter 4, Mike Taylor and Paul Keown examine how teachers can deepen students' thinking about viewpoints, values, and perspectives, important aspects of social studies education. Returning to Keown's (1998) insight that values and social action have been considered the 'hard bits' of social studies teaching, the authors question whether this perception is true today. Making an important connection to the *thinking* key competency—in particular *critical thinking*—the chapter provides practical suggestions for supporting students at all levels of the curriculum to explore viewpoints, values and perspectives.

In Chapter 5, Carol Mutch, Maria Perreau, Bronwyn Houliston, and Jennifer Tatebe argue that an important aim of social studies is to use social inquiry to build students' awareness of social justice issues. However, this inquiry is often stopped before students are given the opportunity to take authentic social action. The authors propose a model of social inquiry that emphasises social action as the best way to teach about, and teach for, social justice.

In Chapter 6, Rachel Tallon considers how a greater awareness of the emotional dynamics of the classroom can equip teachers to broach sensitive or controversial topics and social action. Three pedagogical complexities and three risks are presented as part of a discussion about the importance of pedagogical approaches that positively acknowledge emotions in social studies. She argues that working with, not against, emotions can produce greater learning.

Social studies provides rich opportunities for multi-literacy learning, as outlined by Pip Hunter in Chapter 7. In particular, four types of literacy are promoted for effective social studies: conceptual understandings; responsiveness to diverse cultural contexts and linguistic diversity; use of multimedia and digital technologies; and critical literacy. Such multi-literacies are vital in young people's life worlds, and appreciating the need for multi-literacy learning reorients understanding of citizenship to their own experiences and perspectives.

Finally, in Chapter 8 Rose Atkins and Peter Rawlins identify strategies and practical examples of ways in which the principles of assessment *for* learning can operate in a social studies context, including suggestions for how students' learning can be validly assessed to inform future learning. Atkins and Rawlins emphasise that the key to maximising the formative potential of assessment in social studies is critical reflection on the information that assessments provide, and then basing 'next step' learning and teaching goals on this information.

Together these chapters provide ideas and strategies to support deep, critical, and active learning in social studies. While social studies educators face a number of challenges as they explore people's participation within a complex, dynamic, and contested society with their students, we also believe that doing this well is hugely rewarding for both teachers and students and we hope this book may contribute towards that.

References

Aitken, G. (2005). The purpose and substance of social studies: Citizenship education possibilities. In P. Benson & R. Openshaw (Eds.), *Towards effective social studies* (pp. 85–112). Palmerston North: ERDC Press.

Benson, P. & Openshaw, R. (1998). (Eds.) *New horizons for New Zealand social studies*. Palmerston North: ERDC Press.

Benson, P. & Openshaw, R. (eds) (2005). *Towards effective social studies*. Palmerston North: ERDC Press.

Brooke, M. (1995). Crippled Curriculum Proposed, *The Dominion*, 27 October.

Catling, S., & Martin, F. (2011). Contesting powerful knowledge: the primary geography curriculum as an articulation between academic and children's (ethno-) geographies. *The Curriculum Journal, 22*(3), 317–335. doi:10.1080/0 9585176.2011.601624

Cogan, J., & Derricott, R. (2000). *Citizenship for the 21st century: An international perspective on education*. London: Kogan Page.

Constututional Advisory Panel. (2013). *A report on a conversation He Kōtuinga Kōrero mō te Kaupapa Ture O Aotearoa*. Retrieved from Wellington: http://www.ourconstitution.org.nz/store/doc/FR_Full_Report.pdf

Department of Education. (1944). *Thomas Report*. Wellington: Author.

Electoral Commission. (2015). *Report of the Electoral Commission the 2014 general election*. Retrieved from http://www.elections.org. nz/events/2014-general-election/election-results-and-reporting/ electoral-commission-report-2014-general

Gilbert, R. (2013). Commentary Social science education; Perrennial challenges, emerging issues and curriculum change. *New Zealand Journal of Educational Studies, 48*(2), 143–155.

Harrison, K. (1998). Social studies in the New Zealand curriculum: Dosing for amnesia or enemy of ethnocentrism? In P. Benson & R. Openshaw (Eds.), *New horizons for New Zealand social studies* (pp. 63–82). Palmerston North: ERDC Press.

Heater, D. (1999). *What is citizenship?* Malden, MS: Polity Press.

Hill, B. (2005, September). The social sciences and curriculum obesity. Paper presented at *SocCon 2005: Interconnections and Directions*, Te Papa, Wellington.

Hunter, P., & Keown, P. (2001). The New Zealand social studies curriculum struggle 1993–1997: An 'insider' analysis. *Waikato Journal of Education, 7*, 55–72.

Gibson, S. E. (2009). *Teaching social studies in elementary schools: A social constructivist approach.* Toronto, Canada: Nelson Education.

Isin, E., & Turner, B. (2007). Investigating citizenship: An agenda for citizenship studies. *Citizenship studies, 11*(1), 5–17.

Keown, P. (1998). Values and social action: Doing the hard bits. In P. Benson & R. Openshaw (Eds.), *New horizons for New Zealand social studies* (pp. 137–159). Palmerston North: ERDC Press.

Kerr, D. (1999). Citizenship education in the curriculum: An international review. *The School Field, X*(3/4). Retrieved from http://www.ibe.unesco.org/fileadmin/user_upload/Curriculum/SEEPDFs/kerr.pdf

Lister, R., Smith, N., Middleton, S., & Cox, L. (2003). Young people talk about citizenship: Empirical perspectives on theoretical and political debates. *Citizenship studies, 7*(2), 235–253.

McLaughlin, T. H. (1992). Citizenship, diversity and education: A philosophical perspective. *Journal of Moral Education, 21*(3), 235–250.

Mutch, C. (1998). *The long and winding road: The development of the new social studies curriculum in New Zealand.* Paper presented at the New Zealand Educational Administration Society Biennial Conference Wellington, New Zealand.

Ministry of Education. (2007). *The New Zealand curriculum.* Wellington: Learning Media.

Ministry of Education. (2015). *National Monitoring Study of Student Achievement: Social Studies 2014 - Overview.* Retrieved from Dunedin: http://nmssa.otago.ac.nz/reports/2014/SStudies_Overview.pdf

Meyer, L. (1998). Preface. In P. Benson & R. Openshaw (Eds.), *New Horizons for New Zealand social studies* (pp. i–iii). Palmerston North: ERDC Press.

Nelson, J., & Kerr, D. (2006). *Active citizenship in INCA countries: Definitions, policies, practices, and outcomes.* London: NFER/QCA. Retrieved from http://www.inca.org.uk/pdf/Active_Citizenship_Report.pdf.

Osler, A., & Starkey, H. (2005). *Changing citizenship: Democracy and inclusion in education.* Maidenhead, UK: Open University Press.

Openshaw, R. (1992). (Ed.). *New Zealand social studies: Past, present and future.* Palmerston North: Dunmore Press.

Openshaw, R. (1998). Citizen who? The debate over economic and political correctness in the social studies curriculum. In P. Benson & R. Openshaw (Eds.), *New horizons for New Zealand social studies* (pp. 19–42). Palmerston North: ERDC Press.

Ross, E. W. (1985). *The evolution of the relationship between reflective inquiry and social studies education: Implications for the future*. Paper presented at the National Council for the Social Studies Annual Meeting, Chicago.

Ross, A. (2012). Editorial: Education for active citizenship: Practices, policies and promises. *International Journal of Progressive Education, 8*(3), 7–14. Retrieved from http://inased.org/v8n3/ijpev8n3.pdf

Ross, W., & Marker, P. (2005). Social studies: Wrong, right or left? A critical response to the Fordham Institute Where did Social Studies go wrong? *The Social Studies, July/August*, 139–141.

Thrupp, M., & White, M. (2013). *Research and Analysis into National Standards (RAINS) Project: Final report: National standards and the damage done*. Retrieved from: http://researchcommons.waikato.ac.nz/handle/10289/8394

UNESCO. (2014). *UNESCO Education Strategy: 2014-2021*. Paris: Author. Retrieved from http://unesdoc.unesco.org/images/0023/002312/231288e.pdf.

Wood, B. E. (2013). What is a social inquiry? Crafting questions that lead to deeper knowledge about society and citizenship participation. *set: Research Information for Teachers, 3*, 20–28.

Wood, B. E., & Milligan, A. (2016). Citizenship education in New Zealand: Policy and practice. *Policy Quarterly, 12*(3), 65–73. Retrieved from http://igps.victoria.ac.nz/publications/files/156006894e5.pdf

Wood, B. E., Milligan, A., & Morgan, J. (2013). Special issue, Guest Editorial: Emerging issues and research in New Zealand social science education. *New Zealand Journal of Educational Studies, 48*(2), 2–4.

Young, M., & Muller, J. (2010). Three educational scenarios for the future: Lessons from the sociology of knowledge. *European Journal of Education, 45*(1), 11–27.

Chapter 1 What is this subject called social studies?

Jane Abbiss, with Hilary Kingston

Key points

- Social studies is a contested field and there is confusion about the nature of the school subject.
- Social studies is an integrated subject that draws on the disciplinary traditions of interpretive social sciences, and students of social studies need access to knowledge of multiple disciplines in order to understand social issues.
- Social studies education makes a contribution to disciplinary knowledge through an emphasis on understanding the contested nature of social issues (exploration of values and perspectives), how people adjudicate between different values and actions (engaging in social decision making), and the ways in which people can contribute to social change (through social action).
- Teaching and learning in social studies in New Zealand have developed to focus on conceptual understandings (big or significant ideas) and social inquiry.
- Challenges for social studies educators relate to the negotiation of a conceptual curriculum and shifting teacher–student relationships in

the translation of the curriculum into practice and to support deeper learning in social studies.

Introduction

"What is social studies? I still don't really understand what it is about." This question was posed by a Year 9 student at the end of her first week at a New Zealand high school in 2015. It is a real student, and a real question. And this student has got to the nub of the matter with a simple query. What is social studies? What is it about?

Social studies is a core subject for Years 1 to 10 in New Zealand schools. It is positioned as the foundation for learning in senior social sciences, which include the established school subjects of history, geography and economics (Ministry of Education, 2007). The subject has held this position within the New Zealand school curriculum since the Thomas Report (Consultative Committee on the Post Primary Curriculum, 1944) and education reforms of the 1940s (Mutch, Hunter, Milligan, Openshaw, & Siteine, 2008). It also sits alongside a broad range of social sciences subjects that may be offered in schools in Years 11 to 13. Students can be assessed against social studies achievement standards for the New Zealand Certificate of Educational Achievement (NCEA), the national qualification for secondary schooling (New Zealand Qualifications Authority, n.d.). Yet social studies is a subject that has students, parents and teachers asking, "What is it?"

The starting point for this chapter is that social studies is a legitimate school subject, with knowledge foundations and associated pedagogies, and that it is no less important than English, science or mathematics as a foundation for knowing about the world. The knowledge foundations of social studies are examined with a view to developing an understanding of what social studies is about. In considering the knowledge foundations of the subject, challenges are presented to educators about their roles in shaping the subject and supporting students to understand the contested nature and purpose of social studies.

Knowledge foundations of social studies

When thinking about the disciplinary foundations of social studies, it is important first to clarify just which of the possible 'social studies' is the focus for discussion, because 'social studies' describes different things in different schooling jurisdictions. For example, in the United States 'the social studies' is an umbrella term for a range of subjects, including history and geography, whereas in New Zealand 'social studies' is a subject under a broader umbrella of 'social sciences', along with history, geography, economics and other social science subjects. A learning area called 'social sciences' was first described in the New Zealand curriculum in the early 1990s with the publication of the *New Zealand Curriculum Framework* (Ministry of Education, 1993). Social studies as a subject taught in schools preceded that curriculum.

Social studies, the subject, in New Zealand had its origins in the progressive and new social studies movements of the 1940s and 1960s, respectively. These movements supported social education in the younger years of schooling that drew on a range of social sciences disciplines (including history, geography, sociology, economics and political science) and emphasised ideas such as democratic citizenship and inquiry learning (Aitken 2006; Barr, 1993; Mutch et al., 2008). In different contexts one or different combinations of social studies traditions may have precedence in the curriculum in practice. Four traditions identify social studies variously as: (1) citizenship transmission and education for effective citizenship; (2) social science inquiry; (3) reflective inquiry and decision-making; and (4) personal, social and ethical development (Mutch et al., 2008). The knowledge foundations of social studies can be understood, then, in relation to broad social science disciplinary foundations, international movements, and local subject-specific curriculum developments.

Academic disciplines provide the "means for generating and systematising knowledge" (Brophy, Alleman, & Halvorsen, 2013, p. 54). A subject or discipline has "its own fund of acquired information and a specialized method of inquiry, or a strategy of acquiring that knowledge" (Taba, 1962, p. 172). Notwithstanding tensions that may arise from the position of social studies in the New Zealand curriculum over the years, as both a subject in itself and as a subject that is foundational or preparatory for other social science subjects at the senior level (including history, geography and economics), social studies can be seen to have its own multidisciplinary fund of knowledge.

Drawing on the notions of substantive and syntactical knowledge

(Schwab, 1978), social studies *substantive knowledge*[1] relates to accounts and explanations of social developments, change, conflicts or problems. This substantive knowledge will shift as different views of social developments emerge, and as different and particular social issues enter the frame as important or worthy of attention. Also, at any point in time there will be varied and different accounts and explanations of social events and developments. The *syntactical knowledge* of social studies relates to how students of social studies come to know about the social world, through tools inquiry and the nature of evidence and proof that provide the warrant for new knowledge about that world. In social studies, this syntactical knowledge includes an appreciation that learning in social studies is, in essence, an interpretive act; that ideas and understandings about social developments will change as new evidence is garnered, different perspectives are cultivated and older understandings challenged, and as new insights about social issues emerge, given that different understandings and interpretations will always exist.

Social studies, then, is an integrated subject that draws on a range of disciplinary traditions within the interpretive social sciences as well as an international body of scholarly literature (Barr, 1998). At the heart of its aims is the development of citizenship skills, dispositions and understandings. New Zealand's approach to teaching social studies builds on an international body of scholarly literature that argues that the social sciences disciplines should strongly inform the knowledge base of social studies. Despite an uneasy relationship with disciplines and the scepticism of some educators—some people think of social studies as the bastard subject or poor relation to history, geography, economics and other social sciences subjects—social studies does have a clear, interdisciplinary knowledge foundation.

Central to social studies teaching and learning is a focus on conceptual understanding and social inquiry. These elements are explored in the following section. Other and related key elements of social studies teaching and learning—including a focus on social inquiry for social

---

1 Schwab (1978) defines substantive knowledge in terms of the "conceptual devices which are used for defining, bounding, and analyzing the subject matters" (p. 246) of disciplines. Syntactical knowledge relates to the logical structures that disciplines exhibit, including the different methods of verification and justification of conclusions that constitute the structures of disciplines.

action, exploring values and perspectives in relation to social issues, and multi-literacies for future-facing citizens—are more fully elaborated in other chapters in this book.

A conceptual approach

Internationally there has been a movement to adopt conceptual curricula for social studies related to broad ideas (as opposed to curricula for content prescription). Writing in the 1960s and an early proponent of a conceptual curriculum, Taba (1962) distinguished four levels of knowledge in school subjects: (1) specific facts and processes, (2) basic ideas and principles, (3) concepts, and (4) thought systems. Working towards a new approach for social studies curriculum design, Taba, Durkin, Fraenkel and McNaughton (1971) drew on three of the four levels of knowledge as a foundation for the organisation of social studies subject matter: (1) key concepts; (2) significant or main ideas; and (3) specific facts and cases, or content samples "that serve as samples through the analysis of which students could arrive at the important ideas" (p. iv) and which take the form of in-depth studies of human behaviour. A new approach to social studies curriculum based on conceptual understanding was advocated as an alternative to curriculum that emphasised mastery of facts. Factual knowledge, although relevant to learning in a subject, was seen to be limited because it does not produce new ideas and may have a limited life span as 'facts' are disproved with time. Instead, concepts and basic ideas were seen as a more durable and meaningful foundation for social studies curriculum, teaching and learning.

Concepts represent "complex systems of highly abstract ideas which can be built only by successive experiences in a variety of contexts" (Taba, 1962, p. 178) and which "serve as threads weaving through many grade levels" (Taba et al., 1971, p. iii). In social studies, for example, the concepts of social justice, interdependence, social control or cultural change might present recurrent themes to be developed at different times, in different years and topic contexts, to support the development of an increasingly complex understanding of the social world. Significant ideas include an understanding of causal relationships, such as the laws of science or human culture and natural environment, which constitute important knowledge of the structure of a subject.

These ideas are the fundamentals of a subject, which, despite their contestable nature, are important because "when carefully chosen, they represent the most necessary understandings about a subject or a field and thus constitute in a sense the core curriculum for everyone" (Taba, 1962, p. 177). They represent powerful statements that are significant to the discipline, help with the interpretation of facts and information, and "serve as focal points for the selection and organisation of the content and represent the fundamental learnings" (Taba et al., 1971, p. iv). For example, in studying the interaction between people and their physical environment, learning might be organised around the idea that people in different areas have access to different physical resources, which influences human activity.

Within a conceptual curriculum, contexts of study or topics are selected for the opportunities offered to learners to develop an understanding of the main ideas and concepts:

> It should be possible, for example, to study a few crucial social
> phenomena, such as wars, by asking all the questions a historian
> might ask: what are the factors that create wars; how are wars
> affected by conditions, such as the tools of warfare and the political
> institutions that surround them; what is the history of the causation
> of wars, and so on. One might, in other words, conceivably learn the
> essential ways of being a historian without covering all of history.
> (Taba, 1962, p. 180)

In Taba's and others' view, a new concept of fundamentals in curriculum was required, where fundamentals related not to basic ideas and common bodies of factual knowledge but to an understanding of general principles, with the goal of developing deeper conceptual understanding through a range of experiences over time. Young children, Taba argued, could learn concepts as long as the curriculum and teaching were organised to focus on ideas and teachers had knowledge of how concepts are learned. These ideas have been broadly accepted and have influenced social studies curriculum development internationally.

Notwithstanding variations in nomenclature, significant ideas (also referred to as main, big or powerful ideas or conceptual understandings) are advocated as a foundation for teaching and learning in the social studies and are an organising structure for national curricula for social studies in the early 21st century. In the American context, Brophy et al. (2013), for example, argue that it is important that social studies lessons focus on "powerful ideas" (for example, the causes and consequences of conflict), as opposed to trivial or insignificant information (such as lists of dates). The broader goal is to help students develop "connected understandings of how significant aspects of the social system work, how and why they got to be that way over time, how and why they vary across locations and cultures, and what all of this might mean for personal, social, and civic decision making" (p. 60). Gilbert and Hoepper (2014) argue that, in the Australian context, a goal of teaching within the humanities and social sciences is "deep learning rather than knowledge of information" (p. 8), and that key to this is the explicit identification and teaching of concepts and theories that give disciplines their explanatory power and the application of these concepts to solving problems through inquiry. Deep learning and a focus on big ideas is not something that can be done only in the later years of schooling, but something that can and should be achieved at all levels, with teacher guidance and through processes that support students of all ages to engage with social challenges.

In the New Zealand context, similar support has been given to the teaching and learning of concepts and conceptual understanding in social studies (see, for example, Aitken & Sinnema, 2008; Barr, Graham, Hunter, Keown, & McGee, 1997; Ministry of Education, 2009). Milligan and Wood (2010) support teaching and learning in social studies based on conceptual understandings, while cautioning against seeing conceptual understandings as learning end points. Rather, they suggest, conceptual understandings may be more usefully regarded as learning transition points. A concept-led approach to teaching and learning is advocated, in part, because it "enables teachers to sift and sort through a huge amount of knowledge and start to define 'what counts'" and "helps mitigate the 'mile wide and inch deep' criticism so often directed at social studies" (p. 490). With a broad range of topics and information available to be drawn on and incorporated in social studies programmes, there is a risk in a content-focused approach of superficiality of learning. A concept-focused approach encourages a reduction in coverage in order to teach in greater depth, for deeper understanding and linkages between learning in different topics and contexts.

Turning to consider *The New Zealand Curriculum* (*NZC*), which provides the nationally mandated guide for social studies, the purpose of learning in social studies[2] can be discerned from aspirational statements of moral purpose and through conceptual understandings articulated in the descriptors of the conceptual strands (which have connections to disciplinary foundations) and the achievement objectives specified for curriculum levels 1 (Years 1 and 2) to 8 (Year 13). A range of concepts and big ideas for learning in social studies can be derived from these curriculum elements. These include the causes and consequences of historical and current events, social conflicts or issues; the significance of events, people, places and social developments; the nature of social relationships, interactions, diversity and social change; how people express and maintain their culture, heritage and identity; how people participate in society, exercise social roles and responsibilities, and effect social change; the nature of social structures and the ways in which societies influence and control people; the co-existence of different values and beliefs; and the contestability of different ideas, perspectives and interpretations of social phenomena.

Many of the conceptual elements for social studies learning that are evident in the *NZC* echo ideas from international literature about contemporary social studies curriculum, teaching and learning (Brophy et al., 2013; Gilbert & Hoepper, 2014). Drawing on the notion of concepts as abstract and unifying threads across levels, conceptual threads are discernible across the *NZC* social studies strands and levels relating to cultural diversity, interaction, social change, conflict, social control, interdependence, justice and sustainability—among a range of concepts and not limited to this selection. Moreover, the strand headings can themselves be seen as unifying concepts: identity, culture and organisation; place and environment; continuity and change; and the economic world. The relatively recently produced senior subject guidelines (Ministry of Education, 2013) identify seven concepts in senior social studies, for Levels 6, 7 and 8 (Years 11 to 13): society, culture, change, perspectives, rights, values, and social justice. What New

---

2 There are two official policy documents that make up the New Zealand national curriculum: the English-medium New Zealand Curriculum, and the Māori-medium Te Marautanga o Aotearoa (http://nzcurriculum.tki.org.nz/The-New-Zealand-Curriculum). The English-medium curriculum is the focus of this chapter.

Zealand students should know in social studies is officially defined through these collections of concepts and associated conceptual understandings, albeit with variations in the collections of 'specified' concepts evident in the different policy documents.

Although there has been broad acceptance of the value of a concept-based curriculum, the specific form of the New Zealand curriculum for social studies has been subject to critique. These critiques relate, broadly, to the clarity and coherence of social studies curricula (e.g. Milligan & Wood, 2010) and the relationship between social studies and senior social sciences subjects (including Aitken, 2006). Milligan and Wood (2010) argue that there is a lack of conceptual clarity in social studies teaching and learning, which "may be attributable in part to the ill-defined nature of 'concept' and 'conceptual understanding' in successive social studies curricula" (p. 489), and a lack of specific directives regarding the progressive development of the understanding of concepts across the years and levels of social studies education. The conceptual foundations of social studies in the *NZC* are clear, then, although there appears to be some way to go to clarify conceptual progressions and what it means to teach for conceptual understanding.

Social inquiry

Along with a growing focus on big ideas, emphasis has also been given to social inquiry as a warrant for social studies knowledge. Wood (2013), drawing on the work of Hill (1994) and others, explains how social inquiry emerged in the 1960s with the evolution of a 'social science' discipline that encompassed, but was distinct from, the discrete disciplines of the social sciences. Social inquiry methodologies provided a means of giving the social science discipline intellectual rigour and status.

Social studies evolved in a way that gave greater priority and attention to personalised and action-oriented inquiry related to social challenges in the real world. Inquiry pedagogy, through which students engage in authentic and personally meaningful learning, has its roots in the progressive education movement and the ideas of educational philosopher John Dewey. He wrote about the importance of curiosity, interest and identification with topics in supporting learning, and of direct personal experience and empirical observation in shaping understanding (Dewey, 1916, 1963). For Dewey, the potentialities of education are realised when education "is treated as intelligently directed development of the possibilities inherent in ordinary experience" (1963, p. 89). He argued that "[any study] whether arithmetic, history, geography, or one of the natural sciences, must be derived from materials which at the outset fall within the scope of ordinary life-experience" (p. 73), and for the transformation of classroom methods to recognise the function of interest and experience in supporting learning. In supporting conceptual curricula for social studies, curriculum theorists (including Taba) have simultaneously advocated for an emphasis on conceptual understanding and active, creative and discovery (inquiry) modes of learning. Building understanding of social phenomena and challenges is achieved through explicit teaching of concepts and skills that encourage students to ask questions, conduct inquiries and address problems that are related to real situations and events, explore different perspectives and experiences, and generate (tentative) solutions or responses (Gilbert & Hoepper, 2014).

The guidelines for social studies in the *NZC* assume that social studies is not confined to the ideas of knowing *about* social phenomena (substantive knowledge) but include knowing *through* tools of social inquiry (syntactical knowledge)—what it means to undertake social inquiry and engage with values and perspectives on issues, make considered decisions on possible and preferred actions, and potentially take personal or collective action on an issue. Beyond a focus on particular achievement objectives and New Zealand as a context for learning, and specific references to Māori as tangata whenua (Level 2), Polynesian and British migrations (Level 3) and the Treaty of Waitangi (Level 5), the contexts for learning are open. This reflects principles of flexible and local (teacher-led) curriculum design within the boundaries established by a conceptual national curriculum, which enables teachers to draw on social contexts that are of interest and relevance for learners through subject-based, cross-subject or integrated learning (Ministry of Education, 2009). Notwithstanding concerns about abstraction and a lack of guidance given by the *NZC* about content and social studies learning progression across the levels, and criticism of the downplaying of bicultural elements and content in the revised curriculum, the flexibility of content supports social inquiry relating to social challenges that are meaningful for learners and relevant to their lives and communities.

There are, though, theory–practice negotiations in teaching for social inquiry that derive from questions of agency. Gilbert (2013) contends that the value of social sciences education "must be judged by its contribution to the intellectual and moral wellbeing of our society and its support of people in creating a world which enhances their lives and those of others" (p. 150). The value of social sciences thus relates to agency and social contribution as well as academic or intellectual worth. Writing about agency and 'acts' of history, which is relevant to learning in social studies, Barton argues that "students need to understand that history is made when they engage in the dramatic transformation of public life, but also when they make decisions in their personal lives that affect other people, both near and far" (p. 135). Learning in social studies, then, should be about personal acts and agency, as well as being about developing a deeper understanding of the individual and collective actions of others, past and present. Understanding historical acts, in Barton's view, is strengthened when the concept of agency is explicitly explored and when the human actors with the power to effect actions are not obscured by references to the nations or institutions as the agents of particular acts. Social inquiry, then, needs to support learners to both expand their substantive knowledge of social phenomena and to engage with and adjudicate on values and actions, with a view to understanding and enabling collective and personal options for social action. (See Chapters 3 and 5 for more discussion on approaches to social inquiry and social action.)

Social studies, through social inquiry, supports citizenship aspirations by supporting students to engage with real-life social issues, and to adjudicate on different values, perspectives and actions, and on ways in which people can contribute to social change. This is consistent with an active view of citizenship whereby "democratic citizens are expected to engage in thoughtful, reasoned judgement, individually and collectively, in order to reach well-informed decisions that form the basis for actions" (Barton, 2012, p. 132).

The integrated nature of social studies and the focus on social inquiry is also consistent with the aspirations of 21st century or future-oriented education, characterised by inquiry-based, personalised, collaborative, authentic learning that addresses real-world challenges and makes connections to students' lives (Abbiss, 2015; Bolstad et al., 2012). Arguably, the social inquiry approach helps resolve a tension between deep knowledge in a subject and development of 21st century learning skills, which might be addressed within a subject or as a cross-curricula project. Learning *in* social studies is also important for the development of 21st century skills, competencies and capabilities. Gilbert (2013) encapsulates this argument:

> [I]f these [21st century] skills derive their power and significance from their relevance to contemporary social, economic, political and environmental change, then they can be seen as offering a link between these issues and the traditional knowledge domains of the core curriculum. In other words, by emphasizing an authentic problem-solving approach to contemporary issues, the incorporation of the C21 skills into core curriculum domains will become necessary. (p. 145)

It is through learning in social studies that students engage in deeper learning and knowledge generation and move beyond superficial skills acquisition. Social inquiry supports this deeper form of learning.

Challenges for social studies educators

A range of perennial, curriculum-related challenges and emerging issues need to be negotiated by social studies educators. Gilbert (2013) has described a selection of these in relation to tensions between objectivist approaches to knowledge and subjective elements associated with citizenship and values in action; discipline and subject-based learning and future-oriented education and 21st century skills acquisition; and deep learning and participatory social sciences education. These tensions have been alluded to in this chapter, in relation to social studies education. What also needs to be considered, though, is the role of teachers in the translation of the curriculum in practice.

It has been argued elsewhere that the Social Sciences learning area in the *NZC* presents mixed messages, and that the concepts and conceptual understandings that are identified as the foundation for learning in this area are contestable (Abbiss, 2011). Also, given the permissive and conceptual nature of the curriculum, it is in the *translation* of curriculum signals by teachers that the curriculum and conceptual understandings therein are given meaning for learners. What students learn in social studies thus becomes a matter of teachers' understanding of social studies; that is, teachers' own knowledge, disciplinary background and experience of the subject, their confidence with different topics and potential social studies content, and their values, philosophical views of education and personal sense of moral purpose as social studies educators. Hilarys' story, in the practitioner vignette (below), illustrates a secondary social studies educator's personal journey in relation to her understanding of the subject and how her social studies teaching evolved over time. This vignette challenges teachers to think about how their own biographies influence their social studies teaching and students' experiences and understanding of social studies.

Practitioner vignette: Reflection on teaching social studies— Hilary's story

My experience of social studies at both primary and secondary school was around project learning and topic-based inquiry. I doubt that I would have been able to say what social studies was when I was at primary school. And at secondary school, social studies was a subject on my timetable that I enjoyed but I wouldn't have been able to describe what skills or capabilities I was developing, other than learning facts about different countries and cultures and drawing graphs and maps.

When I started teaching secondary social studies in the late 1990s I worked with prescribed topics and unit plans. My understanding, and what I undoubtedly suggested to my students, was that social studies was an amalgamation of history, geography and economics and was an opportunity to teach (and learn) foundational skills for the three senior disciplines. I started to extend my thinking about social studies teaching and learning when I taught at a school where I was constantly challenged to adapt my teaching approaches to meet the needs and demands of my students. I was further extended and challenged in my thinking about social studies, how to work with a permissive and flexible curriculum and the inextricable links between curriculum and pedagogy, when I had an opportunity to co-facilitate professional learning workshops about the Social Sciences learning area in the revised *NZC* and, more recently, took on the role of full-time social sciences facilitator.

In my experience, the emphasis in professional learning and development initiatives in the last decade has been on developing learner dispositions and engaging in social action through social studies. Teachers have been encouraged to create culturally responsive curricula and to include students, whānau and the community in designing and delivering relevant and inclusive social studies programmes. Through engagement with the revised social sciences curriculum, I came to see that social studies had a broader conceptual focus, with greater emphasis on student-directed learning through the process of inquiry. This encouraged and enabled me to give students greater autonomy in their learning and create opportunities for further depth of student analysis and understanding. For example, where once I would have developed my teaching and learning programme from a list of prescribed topics and learning outcomes, I shifted my practice to co-constructing the learning outcomes and contexts with the students. This enabled students to see themselves and their interests reflected in their learning. The broader themes or concepts from which my teaching and learning programmes were derived better reflected the students', community's and school's vision and values. Greater depth of analysis and learning were achieved through having more flexibility and scope to explore the concepts through multiple contexts. I think that secondary teachers' and students' understandings of what social studies is and appropriate pedagogies have changed for the better—to support more interactive, inquiry-based, authentic and action-oriented learning. However, there is lingering ambiguity about the nature of social studies and how conceptual guidelines might be translated into programmes of study and learning activities in the classroom, with concomitant variations in practice and experiences of social studies teaching and learning.

In reflecting on my experiences, I have become increasingly conscious of my positionality and how my understandings of social studies teaching and learning have been shaped over the years by my own early experiences, my professional role as a secondary teacher, and my personal values about what it is that young people should learn and understand. My biography and values have influenced my curriculum decision making and delivery. Also, I can see that I have been influenced by the potent discourses of subject specialism in the secondary sector, and more recently by the discourses of twenty-first century learning and cultural responsiveness.

I have valued the opportunities I have had to broaden my thinking about social studies. However, policy priorities (where social studies is not considered a priority subject for teacher professional development) mean that it is not always possible for teachers to engage in challenging and cohesive social studies-related professional learning. I wonder, therefore, about how and where teachers might get opportunities to engage with ideas about the nature of social studies and shifting pedagogical practices, and with their own values and beliefs about what is important and relevant in social studies and how these might shape what social studies 'is' for learners in classrooms. Maybe this chapter will invite some teacher-initiated professional conversations about social studies. I hope so.

Teacher disciplinary knowledge and pedagogical content knowledge have been shown to be important factors influencing social studies teaching and learning—in relation to topic selection, the nature of learning opportunities provided for students, and the effectiveness of teaching. For example, Kunowski (2005) found that historical knowledge of the Treaty of Waitangi was central to effective teaching about this required social studies curriculum element: "teachers with this knowledge were able to place events in the context of time and comprehend historical ideas" and "were aware of historical interpretations and the different perspectives from which Māori–Pākehā issues in the past and present can be examined" (p. ii). Similarly, teacher values and moral commitment influence teaching. A moral commitment to biculturalism and recognition of the two cosmologies or cultural landscapes of Aotearoa New Zealand, for instance, support a place-based approach to curriculum design and decision-making (Penetito, 2009). Other teacher values and moral drivers might support different conceptual emphases within curriculum-in-practice in classrooms, such as in relation to conceptual understandings of responsible citizenship, social justice, sustainability and entrepreneurship.

It has been emphasised by scholars who have explored the nature and challenges of future-oriented education that knowing in social studies in the 21st century will be shaped by the nature of the exchange between teachers and learners, and, in the words of Benade (2014), the extent to which teachers are willing and able to "reconceptualise the exchange between themselves and their students" (p. 344). This is not to abandon disciplinary knowledge, nor to relegate the role of the teacher to the periphery of student learning and experience, but to challenge the notion of teaching and learning as a process of knowledge transmission and focus instead on the transformational potential of education and the creation of learning capacity (Bolstad et al., 2012; Gilbert, 2005). As articulated by Bolstad et al. (2012), "disciplinary knowledge should be seen, not as an end in itself, but as a *context* within which students' learning capacity can be developed" (p. 4).

Reconceptualising the exchange between teachers and students in relation to social studies teaching and learning means thinking about how teacher–student power relations may be reconstructed to draw on both teacher and learner strengths and knowledge in the learning process. There is little research that canvasses the nature of social studies teaching and learning in New Zealand classrooms. However, there is some evidence that much—but by no means all—social studies teaching in New Zealand primary and secondary classrooms tends to focus on content and facts rather than on more transformational approaches (Milligan & Wood, 2010; Education Review Office, 2006) and that social inquiry is not well understood by teachers (Wood, 2013). This suggests persistent differences in educators' understanding of the nature and purpose of social studies and the construction of the social studies curriculum in practice. There is, then, an ongoing challenge for social studies educators, in schools and teacher education in particular, to engage with the deeper learning of social studies, based on conceptual understanding and social inquiry, and the nature of teacher–student relationships and how these help to define social studies for learners.

Conclusion

What students should know in social studies is contestable. The social world is complex and the possible content or contexts for learning in social studies are wide ranging. However, the conceptual approach and social inquiry pedagogy advocated in the current New Zealand national curriculum, the *NZC*, are a strong indication of the disciplinary underpinnings of the subject within the social sciences. A continued commitment to an integrated approach to social studies—maintaining links with and drawing on a range of the disciplinary knowledge—recognises the complexity of contemporary society. In other words, students need access to multiple disciplines in order to understand social issues.

Social studies, though, is a subject with its own unique flavour. What social studies education adds to disciplinary knowledge is an emphasis on understanding the contested nature of social issues (through exploration of values and perspectives), how people adjudicate between different values and actions (engaging in social decision making), and the ways in which people, including young people in contemporary New Zealand, can contribute to social change (through social action).

Finding a shared understanding in response to the question 'What is social studies about?' is not so much about educators agreeing on the prescription of social studies content but more about them negotiating what is important and relevant for learners in particular social and cultural contexts, and how students might engage with authentic social issues or problems through social inquiry. In order for educators to be able to articulate and explain to learners what social studies is about, they first need to engage with the question themselves. This chapter is intended to be a stimulus for that conversation.

Reflective questions

- How do you answer the question 'What is social studies?' What different responses to this question exist within your class, syndicate or department?

- How deeply do you embed *syntactical knowledge*, or the tools of social inquiry, into your teaching?

- What, in your mind, is the connection between disciplinary knowledge and social issues?

- How, in your own life and experience, has disciplinary knowledge helped you to understand social issues?

References

Abbiss, J. (2011). Social sciences in the New Zealand Curriculum: Mixed messages. *Curriculum Matters, 7*, 118–137.

Abbiss, J. (2015). Editorial: Future-oriented learning, innovative learning environments and curriculum: What's the buzz? *Curriculum Matters, 11*, 1–9.

Aitken, G. (2006). Signalling shifts in meaning: The experience of social studies curriculum design. *Curriculum Matters, 2*, 6–25.

Aitken, G., & Sinnema, C. (2008). *Effective pedagogy in social sciences / Tikanga ā iwi: Best evidence synthesis iteration*. Retrieved from https://www. educationcounts.govt.nz/publications/series/2515/32879/35263.

Barr, H. (1993). Survival in the South Pacific: The new social studies in New Zealand. *Social Studies, 84*(4), 178–181.

Barr, H. (1998). The nature of social studies. In P. Benson & R. Openshaw (Eds.), *New horizons for New Zealand social studies* (pp. 103–120). Palmerston North: ERDC Press.

Barr, H., Graham, J., Hunter, P., Keown, P., & McGee, J. (1997). *A position paper: Social studies in the New Zealand school curriculum*. Hamilton: University of Waikato. Retrieved from http://nzcurriculum.tki.org.nz/ content/download/569/4032/file/social-studies-positions.doc.

Barton, K. (2012). Agency, choice and historical action: How history teaching can help students think about democratic decision making. *Citizenship Teaching and Learning, 7*(2), 131–142.

Benade, L. (2014). Knowledge and educational research in the context of 'twenty-first century learning'. *European Research Journal, 13*(3), 338–349.

Bolstad, R., & Gilbert, J., with McDowall, S., Bull, A., Boyd, S., & Hipkins, R. (2012). *Supporting future-oriented teaching and learning: A New Zealand perspective*. Report prepared for the Ministry of Education. Wellington: Ministry of Education. Retrieved from http://www.educationcounts.govt.nz/publications/schooling/109306.

Brophy, J., Alleman, J., & Halvorsen, A.-L. (2013). *Powerful social studies for elementary students* (3rd ed.). Belmont, CA: Wadsworth, Cengage Learning.

Consultative Committee on the Post Primary Curriculum. (1944). *The post-primary school curriculum: Report of the committee appointed by the Minister of Education in November, 1942*. Wellington: Government Printer.

Dewey, J. (1916). *Democracy and education: An introduction to the philosophy of education*. New York, NY: McMillan Company.

Dewey, J. (1963). *Experience and education*. Kapa Delta Pi lecture series. New York, NY: Collier Books.

Education Review Office. (2006). *The quality of teaching in years 4 and 8: Social studies*. Retrieved from http://www.ero.govt.nz/National-Reports/The-Quality-of-Teaching-in-Years-4-and-8-Social-Studies-June-2006/Executive-summary.

Gilbert, J. (2005). *Catching the knowledge wave: The knowledge society and the future of education*. Wellington: NZCER Press.

Gilbert, R. (2013). Social science education: Perennial challenges, emerging issues and curriculum change. *New Zealand Journal of Educational Studies*, *48*(2), 143–155.

Gilbert, R., & Hoepper, B. (2014). *Teaching humanities and social sciences: History, geography, economics and citizenship in the Australian curriculum* (5th ed.). South Melbourne, VIC: Cengage Learning.

Hill, B. (1994). *Teaching secondary social studies in a multicultural society*. Melbourne, VIC: Longman Cheshire.

Kunowski, M. (2005). *Teaching about the Treaty of Waitangi: Examining the nature of teacher knowledge and classroom practice*. Unpublished doctoral thesis, Griffith University. Retrieved from https://www120.secure.griffith.edu.au/rch/file/e695f790-13de-1d25-932d-d4175d654f8a/1/02Whole.pdf.

Milligan, A., & Wood, B. (2010). Conceptual understandings as transition points: Making sense of a complex social world. *Journal of Curriculum Studies*, *42*(4), 487–501.

Ministry of Education. (1993). *The New Zealand curriculum framework*. Wellington: Learning Media.

Ministry of Education. (2007). *The New Zealand curriculum*. Wellington: Learning Media.

Ministry of Education. (2009). *Building conceptual understandings in the social sciences: Approaches to building conceptual understandings*. Wellington: Learning Media.

Ministry of Education. (2013). *New Zealand curriculum guides: Senior secondary: Senior social studies*. Retrieved from http://seniorsecondary.tki.org. nz/Social-sciences/Senior-social-studies.

Mutch, C., Hunter, P., Milligan, A., Openshaw, R., & Siteine, A. (2008). *Understanding the social sciences as a learning area: A position paper*. Wellington: Ministry of Education.

New Zealand Qualifications Authority. (n.d.). *Social studies subject resources*. Retrieved from http://www.nzqa.govt.nz/qualifications-standards/ qualifications/ncea/subjects/ social-studies/levels/.

Penetito, W. (2009). Place-based education: Catering for curriculum, culture and community. *New Zealand Annual Review of Education*, *18*, 5–29.

Schwab, J. (1978). Education and the structure of the disciplines. In I. Westbury & N. J. Wilkof (Eds.), *Science curriculum & liberal education: Selected essays* (pp. 229–272). Chicago, IL: University of Chicago Press.

Taba, H. (1962). *Curriculum development: Theory and practice*. New York, NY: Harcourt, Brace & World.

Taba, H., Durkin, M., Fraenkel, J., & McNaughton, A. (1971). *Teachers' handbook for elementary social studies: An inductive approach* (2nd ed.). Reading, MA: Addison-Wesley Publishing Company.

Wood, B. (2013). What is social inquiry?: Crafting questions that lead to deeper knowledge about society and citizenship. *set: Research Information for Teachers*, *3*, 20–28.

Chapter Two Te whanaketanga o te wāhanga ako o te Tikanga ā Iwi: Mai i te kore, ki te wheiao, ki te ao mārama

The development of the Tikanga ā Iwi learning area: From nothingness, to half-light, to the full light of day

Hēmi Dale

Key points

- The development of Māori-medium curricula since the early 2000s has enabled greater expression of Māori self-determination.
- Universal conceptions of citizenship conflict with indigenous people's right to self-determination.
- Tikanga ā Iwi supports students to stand tall in the Māori and wider world, critically shaping society in informed and constructive ways.

Kupu whakataki: Introduction

One retelling of the separation of Ranginui and Papatūānuku suggests that it was Tāne who first saw and experienced the phenomenon of light. His parents, who were locked in an eternal embrace, moved momentarily, allowing a chink of light into a world of abject darkness, a light that was visible only to Tāne. The concept of light proved incomprehensible to his siblings, who were familiar only with darkness. The notion of light was not lost, however, but was passed down to successive generations of Tāne. Eventually the time arrived when Tāne's siblings were prepared to countenance the possibility that the phenomenon of light could be a reality for the world. With collective will and action an enlightened world, te ao mārama, became a reality.

The early 1990s provided another chink of light for te ao Māori when the opportunity arose to produce parallel Māori-medium curriculum statements for each of the essential learning areas of the national curriculum, which would sit alongside their English-medium counterparts with equal mana. Prior to this, the history of curriculum in New Zealand schools had largely been one focused on Western knowledge and delivered through the medium of the English language. Māori knowledge, when evident at all, tended to be at the periphery or an add-on.

In this chapter the development of the Tikanga ā Iwi learning area will be told as a narrative that will illuminate the political nature of Māori-medium curriculum development and its relationship to the wider aspirational goals of te ao Māori. The connection of Tikanga ā Iwi to Social Sciences education, together with some of its points of uniqueness (including te ia o te tikanga ā iwi, or social literacy), will also be discussed.

Te horopaki tōrangapū mō te whanaketanga o ngā marautanga Māori: The political context for Māori-medium curriculum development in the 1990s

The term 'Māori-medium education' refers to those programmes where te reo Māori is the medium of instruction for at least 50 percent of the time, and the goal is to produce learners who are bilingual and biliterate. In Aotearoa, Level 1 Māori-medium schools are categorised as those who use te reo Māori as the language of instruction for 81 to 100 percent of the time, and Level 2 Māori-medium schools use te reo Māori between 51 and 80 percent of the time. The genesis of Māori-medium curricula in the 1990s was a response to the need to produce an educational framework and infrastructure to support and guide the development of Māori-medium schooling that had begun with the emergence of kōhanga reo in the early 1980s, and thereafter kura kaupapa Māori and immersion schools.

Māori-medium curriculum development occurred within the wider context of Māori political development. Durie (1997, 2005) has identified the following key themes:

- Māori–Crown relationships and the Treaty of Waitangi, including Treaty settlements and debates on the bicultural nature of Aotearoa New Zealand and Māori self-determination (tino rangatiratanga)

- iwi development that incorporates the notion of tribal development as a vehicle for Māori advancement, integral to which was the development of a Māori economic base

- the achievement of social equity for Māori through iwi–state partnerships and iwi-driven social delivery systems that would reduce state dependency

- Māori educational advancement through language and cultural revitalisation and Māori educational systems.

The foundation for the initial marautanga, or Māori-medium curricula, was the 1992 *New Zealand Curriculum Framework* (Ministry of Education 1993). This was directly translated by Kāterina Te Heikōkō Mataira and became *Te Anga Marautanga o Aotearoa* (Ministry of Education, 1994). Arohia Durie (2003), in critiquing *Te Anga Marautanga o Aotearoa*, argued that a translated document, however good the translation, is not the same as a curriculum based on Māori values and drawn from Māori knowledge frames. Although this observation is accurate, the important point was the way in which *Te Anga Marautanga* gave rise to a new space for contestation of curriculum to occur and provided the springboard from which the various marautanga were launched.

'Te hīkoi i runga i ngā tapuwae o ngā kaituhi o ngā marautanga reo Pākehā': Walking in the footsteps of the English-medium writers

According to Apple (2014), the development of curriculum is an inherently political process, which prioritises important knowledge over less important knowledge. Liz McKinley, a co-writer of the pūtaiao

(Māori-medium science) curriculum, described pūtaiao's development as both a contestation and a negotiation in relation to selecting what knowledge got included, what knowledge got de-emphasised, and what knowledge fell off.

Somewhat paradoxically, the opportunity for curriculum contestation that the development of the Māori-medium curriculum offered was initially met with caution, if not scepticism, by some Māori educators. The process of developing the parallel curriculum was described as "Te hīkoi i runga i ngā tapuwae o ngā kaituhi o ngā marautanga reo Pākehā", which may be translated as "Walking in the footsteps of the English-medium curriculum writers". This criticism arose from the observation that the writing of each Māori-medium curriculum would begin some 9 months to a year after the English-medium writers had begun writing their particular curriculum document. Whatever else 'parallel' meant, it did not mean starting writing at the same time as the English-medium group (see Papatau 2.1).

The implication was that the initial marautanga Māori (Māori-medium curricula) were empty vessels that amounted to little more than Māori translations of their English-medium curriculum equivalents. As a result, some chose to disengage from the process by withdrawing from curriculum writing groups. However, others continued to engage in the process of curriculum development in the belief that Māori-medium curricula were necessary pou (foundational supports) for the continuing evolution of te whare mātauranga Māori (the Māori-medium educational framework). What is incontrovertible is that the initial process of writing the parallel Māori-medium curriculum was a politically constrained one. There was a tacit expectation that the term 'parallel Māori medium curriculum' meant a 'good' translation of the English-medium curriculum document.

As the principal writer of one of the Māori-medium curricula, and having talked with other principal writers, it is my view that we were all committed to writing curricula that were Māori in both intent and content. Writer resistance and agency proved to be the key strategies by which the political process was redirected to enable the realisation of Māori aspirations such that Māori parallel curricula would be Māori in ethos and, at the very least, parallel, if not superior, to their English-medium counterparts.

Papatau 2.1: Te whanaketanga o ngā marautanga Māori

Table 2.1: Development timeline of the parallel Māori medium curricula

English-medium curriculum	Māori-medium curriculum
1993: The New Zealand Curriculum Framework	1994: Te Anga Marautanga o Aotearoa
1993: Science in the New Zealand Curriculum	1994: Pūtaiao i roto i te Marautanga o Aotearoa
1992: Mathematics in the New Zealand Curriculum	1996: Pāngarau i roto i te Marautanga o Aotearoa
1994: English in the New Zealand Curriculum	1996: Te Reo Māori i roto i te Marautanga o Aotearoa
1995: Technology in the New Zealand Curriculum	1999: Hangarau i roto i te Marautanga o Aotearoa
1997: Social studies in the New Zealand Curriculum	2000: Tikanga ā Iwi i roto i te Marautanga o Aotearoa
2000: The Arts in the New Zealand Curriculum2000	Ngā Toi i roto i te Marautanga o Aotearoa
1999: Health in the New Zealand Curriculum2000	Hauora i roto i te Marautanga o Aotearoa (Tauira)

The following timeline shows the development of the Tikanga ā Iwi curriculum from its beginnings in 1995 through to its modification in 2007, and through to the development of the Māori-medium NCEA[1] Level 1, Level 2 and Level 3 standards for Tikanga ā Iwi, Matawhenua, Ōhanga and Hītori, from 2013 to 2016.

Papatau 2.2: Te rārangi wā mō te whanaketanga o te marautanga Tikanga ā Iwi

Table 2.2: Timeline for the development of the Tikanga ā Iwi curriculum

- **1994:** First draft of social studies curriculum published
- **1995/96:** First draft of Tikanga ā Iwi curriculum written (sandwiched between the writing of draft 1 and draft 2 of the social studies curriculum)
- **1996:** Second draft of social studies curriculum published
- **1997:** Final version of social studies curriculum published
- **Dec. 1997:** First draft of Tikanga ā Iwi curriculum disseminated to schools
- **1998:** National review of first draft of Tikanga ā Iwi curriculum
- **1999:** Second draft of Tikanga ā Iwi curriculum produced.
- **July 2000:** Final version of *Tikanga ā Iwi i roto i te Marautanga o Aotearoa* curriculum published.

---

1   National Certificate of Educational Achievement.

- **2002/03:** Curriculum stocktake
- **2005–07:** Revision of all marautanga (Māori-medium curricula)
- **2008:** Te Marautanga o Aotearoa launched, with Tikanga ā Iwi as one of its eight wāhanga ako (learning areas)
- **2013–16:** Development of Tikanga ā Iwi NCEA Māori-medium Level 1, Level 2 and Level 3 standards

The development of the Tikanga ā Iwi curriculum began in the crossfire that erupted in the mid-1990s between those who supported the bicultural first draft of social studies (which included references to biculturalism, tangata whenua, Pākehā and colonisation) and those who supported the more conservative second draft that made no overt reference to biculturalism and instead typified us all as settlers. The first draft of the Tikanga ā Iwi curriculum became, to some extent, collateral damage in that it was aligned to the second more conservative draft of social studies by virtue of being written at the same time as the second draft. Teacher feedback about the first draft of Tikanga ā Iwi generated a national hui of primary and secondary teachers, who critiqued the first draft. The subsequent report identified a small list of elements of the draft that were valued as well as a very long of list of things that needed to be rethought or rectified. A new writing group was established, who wrote a second draft of Tikanga ā Iwi, which eventually became the final Tikanga ā Iwi document, *Tikanga ā Iwi i roto i te Marautanga o Aotearoa.*

In reconceptualising the Tikanga ā Iwi learning area, this second writing group started in a different head space to that of the first Tikanga ā Iwi writing group. Some of the critical questions that guided the group included:

- Where are Māori located in society? Where do Māori aspire to be?

- What role might Tikanga ā Iwi have in realising these aspirations?

- Is Tikanga ā Iwi culturally and politically neutral, or is it social engineering?

- What might an authentic 'Māori Tikanga ā Iwi curriculum' look like?

- What is meant by social amnesia? How would you know if you were suffering, or not, from this ailment?

- What does effective pedagogy in Tikanga ā Iwi look like?

- How will mātauranga Māori and tikanga Māori be embedded in Tikanga ā Iwi?
- What linguistic challenges need to be mediated by Tikanga ā Iwi?

The Tikanga ā Iwi curriculum that developed was underpinned by the following theoretical foundations.

Papatau 2.1: Te tūāpapa ariā o Tikanga ā Iwi
Figure 2.1: Theoretical underpinnings of Tikanga a Iwi

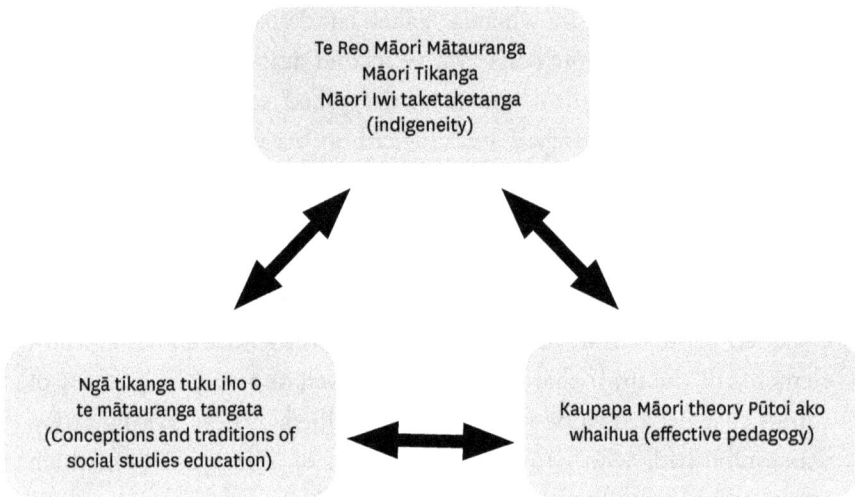

Te Reo Māori Mātauranga Māori Tikanga Māori Iwi taketaketanga (indigeneity)

Ngā tikanga tuku iho o te mātauranga tangata (Conceptions and traditions of social studies education)

Kaupapa Māori theory Pūtoi ako whaihua (effective pedagogy)

Kaupapa Māori theory—with its emphasis on the validity and legitimacy of Māori language, knowledge and culture—and critical theory are an integral part of this foundation. Giroux (1988) argues that the first question before the development of citizenship education or social studies is whether or not society should be changed in a particular way or left as it is. The next step is to raise teacher consciousness about the role of the school in society, to learn that pluralism without an examination of the way the dominant culture controls the others is not enough. Everything needs to be decoded.

Tikanga ā Iwi can be emancipatory so long as it maintains a focus on both analysis and action. The main aim of Tikanga ā Iwi is 'te tū tangata o te ākonga i te ao Māori, i te ao whānui anō hoki kia kaha ai tōna uru mōhiohio, uru haepapa atu ki ngā mahi waihanga porihanga.' (Ministry of Education, 2000, p. 8). The first part of the main aim states that students will stand tall in the Māori world and in the wider world. This is a long-held Māori aspiration. The emancipatory element of the main aim is the final part, which talks of enabling informed students who are constructively critical and able to engage responsibly and in an informed way in shaping society. The subtext is an emphasis on the actualisation of tino rangatiratanga through active citizenship.

Te ia o te tikanga ā iwi: Social literacy

Active citizenship and the notion that enabling students to actively participate in shaping our changing society became the catalyst for the development of a social literacy statement in 1998. The following principles were espoused.

(i) Addressing social amnesia and the 'silences'

- Deliberate and systematic inclusion of Māori content such as tribal and hapū histories, raupatu, the significance of the 1835 Declaration of Independence, indigenous rights, Treaty settlements, language revitalisation, significant individuals such as Meri Mangakāhia, significant historical events such as Takaparawhau.

(ii) To be outward looking

- That there be opportunities to look beyond our own local and national society as a way of understanding more about ourselves as individuals and as a collective.

(ii) Iwi taketaketanga (indigeneity)

- Māori are part of that global indigenous movement and as such are engaging internationally, nationally and at the local level in the realisation of the goal of self-determination.

(iii) Developing a critical view

- That there be opportunity for learners to develop critical literacy skills.
- Ways in which media construct identity, particularly for indigenous groups within a dominant culture.
- Breaking down of stereotypical myths associated with particular groups of people.

(iv) Promote positive and current images of Māori in a range of authentic contexts

- That there is opportunity to explore and examine a range of Māori perspectives on historical and contemporary issues.

(v) To actively engage students in their learning (social inquiry and effective pedagogy)

(vi) To develop a range of perspectives on different issues

- To provide opportunity for learners to explore, examine and challenge their own values positions on a variety of issues and to develop a range of perspectives on different issues.

(vii) To develop understanding of the diversity and complexity of Māori perspectives

- Incorporate and reinforce cultural values and beliefs in traditional and contemporary contexts.

- Recognise that knowledge of Māori language, traditions, histories and values contribute to a Māori world view.

- Critically examine issues, both internal and external, historical and present-day, related to the realisation of Māori social, political, cultural and economic aspirations within Aotearoa.

(viii) Mātauranga Māori me te mātauranga o ētahi (Māori knowledge and the knowledge of others)

- That there be opportunities for learners to access Māori knowledge and also the knowledge of others.

- Tikanga ā iwi will recognise Māori cultural knowledge as a living and constantly adapting system that is grounded in the past, but continues to grow through the present and into the future.

- Tikanga ā iwi will foster a complementary relationship across knowledge derived from diverse knowledge systems.

This last principle, relating to Māori knowledge, was included in the Tikanga ā Iwi curriculum as a pragmatic response to a polarising debate that raged in the 1990s. The debate centred on the recognition of the importance of Māori knowledge. While there was little disagreement about this, the debate was framed as either being pro-mātauranga Māori or anti- mātauranga Māori (that is, pro-mātauranga Pākehā, white man's knowledge). In stigmatising Western knowledge there was no middle ground between the two polarities. Correspondence with other indigenous peoples provided the way forward. The Inuit of Alaska had developed their own cultural standards, which resonated with our own belief system. With their agreement we included a statement in the Tikanga ā Iwi curriculum about the importance of learners having access to their own knowledge, but also the knowledge of others.

Mai i te marautanga Tikanga ā Iwi ki te wāhanga ako o te Tikanga ā Iwi: From Tikanga ā Iwi curriculum to Tikanga ā Iwi learning area

The 2002/03 Curriculum Stocktake led to the review, from 2005 to 2007, of all Māori-medium curricula. A national stakeholder group, Te Ohu Matua, comprising the sector groups and organisations connected to Māori-medium education, oversaw the process of refining the marautanga. A key differentiating feature of the curriculum-writing process at this time, as compared to the process in the 1990s, was the higher level of autonomy evident throughout. Apart from the directive that there must be eight levels, there were effectively no other constraints. The writers of each learning area were able to work as a collective, which ensured both a more collaborative and a more robust process.

The co-ordinated development of curriculum-specific vocabulary across the learning areas, for instance, was the complete opposite of the isolationist vocabulary development approach followed in the 1990s. The Tikanga ā Iwi learning area, like the other learning areas, became a slim-line version of itself but still adhered to the key notions of social literacy and active citizenship that were initially espoused. The essence of the Tikanga ā Iwi learning area is still the acronym MMP. That is, Tikanga ā Iwi programmes need to provide opportunity for learners to develop:

- m̲ōhiotanga (knowledge) with regard to the kaupapa or theme that is being investigated

- m̲āramatanga (understandings) in relation to the conceptual aspect of human behaviour that is being focused on

- **p**ūkenga pakirehua (inquiry skills) while undertaking their Tikanga ā Iwi investigations.

There is also a secondary level of MMP that teachers need to address to ensure authentic Tikanga ā Iwi outcomes. This MMP reads as follows:

- **m**ōhiotanga (knowledge) in relation to the kaupapa being taught and how to connect it to the intent of the marautanga

- **m**āia (brave)—although it is sometimes easier to take the path of least resistance, teachers and schools sometimes need to be brave in regard to the choices they make about what is taught

- **p**ūtoi ako whaihua (effective pedagogy)—ensuring that effective pedagogy underpins learning and teaching in Tikanga ā Iwi inquiry.

Te kirirarautanga mātātoa me te iwi taketaketanga: Active citizenship and indigeneity

Two key underpinnings of the Tikanga ā Iwi curriculum are active citizenship (kirirarautanga mātātoa) and indigeneity (iwi taketaketanga). The two notions are both connected and contested. The terms 'iwi taketake' (indigenous, literally first or original people) and 'tangata whenua' (or people of the land) are both used synonymously as a term for indigenous peoples. Māori are part of the global indigenous movement, and as such are engaging internationally, nationally and at the local level towards the goal of tino rangatiratanga (self-determination). Expressions ranging from the historical 'whakahōnoretia te Tiriti' (honour the Treaty) to the more contemporary 'mā te Māori, mō te Māori' (by Māori for Māori) and 'ki te whakaaro whānui tonu, heoi anō, ki te whakatinana ā rohe tonu" (think globally, but act locally) all give a strong sense of the importance of tino rangatiratanga to the Māori nation.

The Hui Taumata Mātauranga (Māori Educational Summits) in the early 2000s identified the following Māori educational goals:

- to live as Māori

- to participate as citizens of the world

- to enjoy good health and a high standard of living.

Maaka and Fleras (2005) argue that a key element in the realisation of Māori aspirations "to live as Māori, to actively participate as citizens of the world and to enjoy good health and a high standard of living" (Durie, 2003) is the reconciliation of the fundamental tension in Aotearoa between the universal democratic rights of all citizens on the one hand, and indigeneity and the collective rights asserted by Māori as tangata whenua on the other. This tension is both historical and contemporary. They argue that universal citizenship and its emphasis on equal rights and similar privileges for all under a single set of laws is in direct conflict with the principle of indigeneity and indigenous peoples as autonomous peoples with inherent rights to self-determination as tangata whenua. The solution they propose is a form of indigenous citizenship they call "citizenship plus", which recognises collective and inherent rights to self-determination as a framework for "belonging together with our differences in post-colonising societies" (Maaka & Fleras, 2005, p. 42). Goodall (2005) supports the notion of belonging together differently by arguing that the explicit recognition of indigenous rights over the last 20 years has resulted in an economic, political and cultural renaissance that has delivered to Māori "more choice and control over their own destiny than at any time since colonisation in the early 1800s".

Counter discourses have also emerged, such as Rata's contention (2006) that biculturalism is subverting democracy and has led to separatism by setting up ethnic boundaries between Māori and non-Māori. This was exemplified in the Ngāi Tūhoe Treaty settlement with the Crown. Tāmati Kruger, one of Tūhoe's settlement lead negotiators, made reference to Ngāi Tūhoe's dual citizenship; that is, membership of the Tūhoe nation and belonging as a citizen to Aotearoa-New Zealand. This statement was misrepresented by some as Tūhoe's tribal isolationist policy or as a racist separatist movement. More recently, the 2015 Iwi-Kiwi water rights campaign and the subsequent 2016 Hobson's Pledge campaign have focused on ending what they refer to as "Māori privilege" and the descent into a separatist nation. This issue highlights the tension between the universal democratic rights of all citizens on the one hand and indigeneity and the collective rights asserted by Māori as tangata whenua on the other.

The debate around the vexed notion of having Māori seats on the Auckland Council was certainly one that illuminated the tensions that exist between the reconciliation of universal citizen rights and indigenous rights. The eventual decision that having Māori seats would not be in the best interests of fairness and democracy was extremely well satirised by Syd Keepa (2013), in his letter to the editor entitled 'Māori Seats'.

Māori Seats

The debate regarding Māori seats for the proposed Super City's Auckland council makes me wonder that if the boot was on the other foot, would the history-deniers see why Māori are annoyed with their ranting?

Consider if for 200 years the land had been occupied by Pākehā and one day a waka full of Māori then imposed their culture on the Pākehā population, confiscated their land and outlawed their culture to a point where it was almost eliminated. Nearly 70 years later the education system described Pākehā as savages and the only way Pākehā could be saved was to allow Māori to impose their wishes and structures on them.

Te reo was the only official language and Pākehā were denied a vote in the political system, but as a gesture, four Pākehā seats were developed in Parliament so Māori could have some sort of control of national and local governing bodies.

Pākehā place names were changed to Māori names and Pākehā were deprived of their rights as the first people of the land and had to fight for recognition, all this in the space of 200 years—from citizen to second-class citizen.

Syd Keepa, Birkdale. (*New Zealand Herald*, 27 April, 2013, p.10)

The connectedness of te ao Māori and te ao iwi taketake (the indigenous world) is further evidenced in the Māori-medium NCEA Level 1, Level 2 and Level 3 standards, which have an indigenous thread running through the three levels, culminating in a number of indigeneity-focused standards available at Level 3. Ultimately it will be future generations who resolve the tension between active citizenship and indigenous rights here in Aotearoa. While optimistic about how far we have come in the last two decades, the launching of the recent 2016 Hobson's Pledge campaign by Don Brash provides a salutary reminder that we have not yet arrived at 'pae tata' (close horizon) in terms of our political relationship (see Chapter 1 for a discussion on the possibilities within social studies for navigating these contested issues).

Te whanaketanga o te puna kupu o Tikanga ā Iwi: Development of a Tikanga ā Iwi corpus

The development of the Māori-medium curriculum in the 1990s and subsequent iterations thereafter have been a major contributor to the corpus of educational words and terms in the Māori language. This process was initially not co-ordinated, and was in fact rather haphazard. Not until the end of the curriculum writing process was there some limited opportunity for the writers of Tikanga ā Iwi, Ngā Toi and Hauora to discuss the lexical terms being used with a view to achieving some consistency. A particularly good example was the word used for 'investigate'. In one marautanga the word used was 'torotoro' while another used 'tūhura' and attributed another meaning to the word 'torotoro'. Tikanga ā iwi, with the initial support of Te Taura Whiri i te Reo Māori (the Māori Language Commission), advocated 'whakatewhatewha' as the more accurate term. Māori-medium teachers who were the receivers and consumers of these words complained about the volume of the new words to be learnt and also the inconsistency in the usage of some of these words.

The Tikanga ā Iwi curriculum's strategy was a pragmatic one, which included a linguist in our writing group who was also a first-language speaker of te reo Māori. This enabled a more systematic approach to the development of the Tikanga ā Iwi corpus. The use of the sentence 'Kāhore he mea tika, kāhore he mea kotahi' (There is not one but many) also gave a clear message in regard to the accepting and valuing of dialectal words that might be used instead of some of the Tikanga ā Iwi terms while reinforcing the valuing of dialectal words. A number of words have needed to be created to respond to the linguistic needs of the Tikanga ā Iwi learning area. Examples of these words and terms are shown in the following table.

Papatau 2.3: Ētahi o ngā kupu i hangaia mō te marautanga Tikanga ā Iwi

Table 2.3: Some of the Tikanga ā iwi terms developed for the Tikanga ā Iwi learning area

ataata taurite	a stereotype
whakawaimemehatanga	assimilation
whakaurunga	integration
tāmitanga (o te hinengaro)	colonisation
te wetewete i te tāmitanga	decolonisation (literally the unravelling of colonisation)

tāutu(tia/hia)	identify
tautuhi(a)	define
pakirehua pāpori	social inquiry
mōhiohio	information
mōhiotanga	knowledge
māramatanga	understanding
te tīmata panoni	initiating change
te whakauenuku tikanga tuku iho	maintaining cultural practices
te whakarauora reo iwi taketake	revitalising indigenous language
te atawhai i a Papatūānuku	protecting the environment
te hāpai i ngā motika tōrangapū	standing up for political rights

The curriculum review from 2006 to 2008 and the development of the Māori-medium NCEA standards has provided further opportunity for review and standardisation of the curriculum lexicon. Dictionaries have been developed by the Ministry of Education for pāngarau, pūtaiao and ngā toi, and it is hoped that there will be a similar dictionary developed for the Tikanga ā Iwi words and terms that have been developed over the last 20 years.

Te pūtoi ako o te pouako: Teacher pedagogy

In critiquing the second draft of the social studies curriculum, Harrison (1998) argued that it would not unlock the past for New Zealand children. Nor would it

> liberate Pākehā children from stereotyping, misconceptions and discrimination. It would not empower Māori children to name the forces of history that acted brutally on their ancestors and visited misfortune on them. Cultural modification would occur through the forgetting of the past. Those who occupy the ranks of the dispossessed and powerless would not learn the words that explain and expose their position. Those words are colonisation, war and racism.
> (Harrison, 1998, p. 77)

Pat Snedden (2005), in reflecting on national awareness and conscientisation with regard to the Treaty of Waitangi, offers a more optimistic view in arguing that levels of social awareness of Treaty issues have risen dramatically. He cites the singing of the national

anthem in Māori and English as an example of how our cultural practices are adapting. He argues that we now have a huge historical base
to draw on, which is a great advantage provided we see it reflected in
our school system:

> The challenge for the twenty-first century school age child is to gain a
> grasp of the new history written in the last thirty years, by historians
> and through the Tribunal process. (p. 181)

> If the generation since 1975 may be described as the Treaty truth-
> telling generation, let the next be the Treaty fulfilment generation.
> (p.184)

Tikanga ā iwi is an enabling curriculum, but variability of teacher
knowledge and practice can mean that 'he tangata rongonui' (a famous
person) project-type Tikanga ā Iwi work can still be evident in schools.
The tauaromahi Tikanga ā Iwi (Tikanga ā Iwi exemplar project) work
undertaken from 2003 to 2004 provided valuable insight into Māori-
medium teachers' Tikanga ā Iwi practice. Teachers showed good
understanding of the pakirehua (inquiry) part of the pakirehua pāpori
(social inquiry) process. However, finding authentic examples of te
tūhura uara (values exploration) proved very difficult, and te whakatau
kaupapa pāpori (social action) even more difficult. This pattern was
mirrored in the English-medium social studies exemplars. To some
extent this may be attributable to the very limited opportunities for
professional learning and development for teachers in the Tikanga ā
Iwi learning area.

The other key factor that has had an inhibiting effect in terms of
teachers' Tikanga ā Iwi choices is the range of Tikanga ā Iwi resources
available in te reo Māori. It remains problematic that values exploration
and social action—the two unique features at the heart of Tikanga ā
Iwi education—are under-represented in classroom programmes (see
Chapters 4 and 5 for further exploration of values exploration and
social action).

Kupu whakamutunga: Conclusion

An observation by Te Mātorohanga in 1865 is the overarching statement for the Tikanga ā Iwi learning area:

> Kāore i kotahi te whakahaere o ngā Tikanga ā Iwi. He iwi anō me
> ōna tohunga me ōna tikanga me āna whakahaere. Hiki atu he iwi,
> pērā tonu. Nō reira, kia mau koe ki ōu ake .... Mā ō rātou uri e mau
> ō rātou nā kōrero. Engari kia mau koe ki ngā kōrero a ōu mātua, a ōu
> tūpuna. Ina ka tika, ka waiho mai ētahi mātauranga hei taonga mōu.

This text may be translated as follows:

> The organisation of social customs and practices is diverse, not
> unitary. Each people has its own experts, customs and organisational
> structures. It is a pattern that is consistent irrespective of the people.
> Therefore, hold fast to your own ... Let the descendants of others
> retain their own histories and stories. You must retain the collective
> wisdom of your parents and ancestors. If this is done appropriately,
> greater knowledge and wisdom will result.

This statement embodies the wairua (spirit) of the Tikanga ā Iwi learning area in that it makes explicit its Māori identity and connectedness to te ao Māori. In looking outward at other peoples, it alludes to the importance of relationships, including those with other indigenous peoples. Te Mātorohanga's emphasis on the development of knowledge and wisdom resonates with Tikanga ā Iwi's emphasis on the importance of the development of higher-level conceptual knowledge of human behaviour and tikanga. Implicit within the statement is the notion of active critical engagement with the world, whether that be whānau, hapū, iwi or community.

The Tikanga ā Iwi curriculum emerged into the world of light amidst the politics of education of the 1990s. Through resistance and agency it has actualised its own Māori identity within the New Zealand curriculum landscape, and also within the international indigenous curriculum landscape. Māori political advocate Moana Jackson has characterised this identity as 'Our own way of seeing and making sense of the world' (Jackson, 2001). There is still much to be done, however. The biggest challenges are the development of a Tikanga ā Iwi critical mass and creating opportunities for the on-going development of teacher capacity in the Tikanga ā Iwi learning area.

Ētahi pātai whakaaroaro: Reflective questions

- How could the principles of 'social literacy' be used to strengthen Tikanga ā Iwi / social studies programmes at your school/institution?

- To what extent are the main goals of Tikanga ā Iwi reflected in your school's or institution's curriculum planning?

- How do you define citizenship? In what ways does this definition match *universal citizenship* or *citizenship plus*, as defined in this chapter?

- In what ways could it be said that social studies programmes encourage *social amnesia*? How should this be prevented?

Papakupu: Glossary

ataata taurite = a stereotype

hapū = sub-tribe

hītori = history

iwi = tribe or people

iwi taketake = indigenous

iwi taketaketanga = indigeneity

kirirarautanga mātātoa = active citizenship

māia = brave

marautanga = curriculum

matawhenua = geography

ōhanga = economics

pakirehua = inquire, inquiry

pakirehua pāpori = social inquiry

Papatūānuku = Earth Mother

pātai whakaaroaro = reflective questions

pūkenga = skill

Pūtaiao = Māori medium science learning area

pūtoi ako whaihua = effective pedagogy

Ranginui = Sky Father

Tāne (Mahuta) = son of Ranginui and Papatūānuku, guardian of forests and all living things within tangata whenua = people of the land, indigenous people

tauaromahi = exemplar

te ao iwi taketake = the indigenous world

te ao Māori = the Māori world; the Māori nation

te whakatau kaupapa pāpori = social action

tikanga = cultural behaviour or practice, value

Tikanga ā Iwi = Māori medium social sciences learning area

tohunga = expert

tūhura uara = values exploration

Ngā pukapuka i tirohia: References

Apple, M. W. (2014). *Official knowledge: Democratic education in a conservative age.* (3rd Ed.). New York, NY: Routledge.

Durie, A. (2003). Curriculum framing. *set: Research Information for Teachers, 2.* 17.

Durie, M. (1997). *Te mana, te kāwanatanga: The politics of Māori self-determination.* Auckland: Oxford University Press.

Durie, M. (2005). *Nga tai matatu: Tides of endurance.* Auckland: Oxford University Press.

Giroux, H. (1988). *Teachers as intellectuals: Toward a critical pedagogy of learning.* Westport, CT: Bergin & Garvey Publishers.

Goodall, A. (2005). Crown and Māori in Aotearoa—Tai timu, tai pari: The ever-changing tide of indigenous rights in Aotearoa New Zealand. In G. Cant, A. Goodall & J. Inns (Eds.), *Discourses and silences: Indigenous peoples, risks and resistence.* Christchurch: Canterbury University Press.

Harrison, K. (1998). Social studies in the New Zealand curriculum: Dosing for amnesia or enemy of ethnocentrism. In P. Benson & R. Openshaw (Eds.), *New horizons for New Zealand social studies.* Palmerston North: ERDC Press.

Jackson, M. (2001, September). Tikanga ā iwi professional learning and development wānanga. Epsom, Auckland.

Maaka, R., & Fleras, A. (2005). *The politics of indigeneity challenging the state in Canada and Aotearoa New Zealand.* Dunedin: University of Otago Press.

Ministry of Education. (1993). *New Zealand curriculum framework.* Wellington: Learning Media.

Ministry of Education. (1994). *Te anga marautanga o Aotearoa.* Wellington: Learning Media.

Ministry of Education. (2000). *Tikanga ā iwi i roto i te marautanga o Aotearoa.* Wellington: Learning Media.

Ministry of Education. (2008). *Te marautanga o Aotearoa.* Wellington: Learning Media.

Snedden, P. (2005). *Pākehā and the Treaty: Why it's our Treaty too.* Auckland: Random House.

Further reading

Berg-Nordlie, M., Saglie, J., & Sullivan, A. (Eds.). (2015). *Indigenous politics, institutions, representation and mobilisation.* Colchester, UK: ECPR Press.

Gjerpe, K. (2013). *The best of both worlds: Conceptualising an urban Sāmi identity.* Unpublished master's thesis, University of Tromsø, Norway.

McKinley, E. (1995). *The politics of knowledge: Māori and curriculum. in* NAMMSAT (1995) Proceedings of Inaugural NAMMSAT Conference. Auckland University, Te Puni Kōkiri.

O'Sullivan, D. (2007). *Beyond biculturalism: The politics of indigenous minority.* Wellington: Huia Publishers.

Penetito, W. (2010). *What's Māori about Māori education?* Wellington: Victoria University Press.

Sachdeva, S. (2016). 'Anti-separatist' campaign launched against 'Maori favouritism' ahead of 2017 election. Retrieved from http://www.stuff.co.nz/national/politics/84742581/antiseparatist-campaign-launched-against-maori-favouritism-ahead-of-2017-election

Stewart-Harawira, M. (2005). *The new imperial order: Indigenous responses to globalisation.* Wellington: Huia Publishers.

Te Hautaka Mātai Mātauranga o Aotearoa New Zealand Journal of Educational Studies (2012) 47(2). Special Issue: He aha te kaupapa? Critical conversations in Kaupapa Māori. Guest Editors: Te Kawehau Hoskins and Alison Jones, University of Auckland.

Tobin, E. (1996). *Report and recommendations on the bicultural component of the revised draft.* Unpublished report to the Ministry of Education.

Tomlins-Jahnke, H., & Mulholland, M. (Eds.). (2011). *Mana tangata: Politics of empowerment.* Wellington: Huia Publishers.

Chapter 3 Issues-based social inquiry in social studies and citizenship education

Andrea Milligan, Philippa Hunter and Michael Harcourt

Key points

- Social studies and citizenship education deal with significant social, political, cultural, economic and environmental issues and problems. Such issues are open, authentic and contemporary.

- Social inquiry is a key approach for enabling learners to explore issues and their own and others' responses to them.

- Effective issues-based social inquiry enables learners to see nuance and complexity in their social world. Sophisticated understanding involves an appreciation of multiple perspectives, rather than 'two sides of a debate'.

Introduction: Why issues education?

As previously outlined in this book, stormy debate has surrounded questions about the exact rationale and aims for New Zealand social studies and citizenship education. Citizenship itself is a contested concept in education. In this discordant context, the central point of this chapter is that discord itself is the very stuff of social studies and citizenship education. In other words, uncertainty is our core business. To explore this contention further, let's consider two broad aims for social studies and citizenship education: that it enables students to (a) *understand* their social worlds more clearly, by exploring descriptive questions about how society can be characterised, and (b) *participate* in their social worlds, including through the exploration of ethical questions about how society *should be* and taking action (adpated from Barr, 1998).

Notably, both (a) and (b) involve controversy. To understand societies in any meaningful sense is to notice the often persistent controversies borne of pluralism: differences in values, social mores and cultural preferences that are a fact of our social world. Granted, social studies and citizenship education have a legitimate and important role in attending to societal stability; that is, describing "how society works" (Ministry of Education, 2007, p. 30) and the "positive traditions and institutions" that characterise society (Patrick, Vontz, & Nixon, 2002). However, as Nelson (1996) argues,

> pervasive human issues remain at the center of the human condition and at the core of knowledge. The legitimate study of society, human knowledge, and competing views, therefore requires a focus on issues. (p. 14)

Participating in society is also controversial because, unless we blindly replicate the status quo, we must collectively decide how we shall live with others on this Earth. At some level, teachers will shape learners' views about this—education inevitably has its forms of socialisation. However, to be educative, social studies and citizenship education enable students to identify and critically assess a range of options for responding to societal dilemmas and challenges, sometimes described as *counter*-socialisation (Barr, Graham, Hunter, Keown, & McGee, 1997; Ochoa-Becker, 2007). Thus, teaching for social participation not only acknowledges the unresolved aspects of their social worlds, but exposes students to differing ethical visions for how change could be brought about.

Such is the international weight behind issues education, the vast majority of contemporary social studies and citizenship academics "would agree that social studies involves practising problem solving and decision making for developing citizenship skills on crucial social issues" (Barr et al., 1997, p. 39). Issues education has been strenuously advocated on the basis that (i) it enables learners to adapt to society and cope with the complex demands of participating in their social worlds, (ii) it has a transformative dimension, allowing students to define the 'good life' for themselves and their communities, and (iii) controversy is essential to democratic life, and democratic wellbeing depends on a knowledgeable, articulate and politically engaged citizenry (see, for example, Hess, 2004, 2009; Ochoa-Becker, 2007; Shaver, 1992).

What do we mean by issues?

Issues education has had a longstanding, albeit variable, place in social studies and citizenship education internationally. In the United States, and with the associated tradition of social studies taught as reflective inquiry, issues education reaches back to the work of Dewey, the social welfare and humanitarian movements of the early 19th century, and, arguably, to the teachings of Socrates (Evans & Saxe, 1996; Patrick et al., 2002; Saxe, 1992). Often referred to as the 'problems of democracy', two prominent experiments with this approach were the Harvard Social Studies Project and the Crucial Issues in Government series of the 1960s and 1970s. Academic interest in teaching controversial issues in the UK stemmed from the Humanities Curriculum Project in the late 1960s, led by Lawrence Stenhouse (1971), and developments in the 1970s and 1980s (see, for example, Carrington & Troyna, 1988; Dearden, 1981; Stradling, 1984; Wellington, 1986). This body of work saw controversial issues occupying a central place in citizenship education in the UK until a period of curriculum revision in 2013/14 (see, for example, Claire, 2003; Claire & Holden, 2007; Oulton, Day, Dillon, & Grace, 2004). Similarly, Australasian educators have long advocated an issues-based approach to social studies education (see, for example, Aitken, 2005b; Gilbert & Hoepper, 2004; Hill, 1994; Reynolds, 2009).

It is notable that varying definitions and characteristics have been ascribed to issues, different rationales have been advanced for this focus in education (see, for example, Evans & Saxe, 1996; Hess, 2008; Levinson, 2006; Shaver, 1992), and opinion is divided over how central an organising concept 'issues' should be (Patrick et al., 2002). Some, for example, "would advocate the study of only perennial issues while other [sic] emphasize current or personal issues, such as moral dilemmas and values clarification" (Ross, 2006, pp. 22–23).

Two definitions may give readers an indication of the stance taken in this chapter. The New Zealand educator Graeme Aitken (2005b) describes topical, controversial issues as having the following characteristics:

- they involve a specific problem about which different groups in a community urge conflicting courses of action

- they are of such significance that each means of resolution is objectionable to some groups of citizens and arouses protest

- they are concerned with value judgements and therefore cannot be settled on facts and evidence alone

- they involve participants in a decision-making process. (p. 102)

Issues that motivate young people are often observable, particularly through digital sources and social media networks, and focus on real people with the capacity to act, or otherwise, when seeking or resisting change. Aitken (2005b) continues:

> They also need to have relevance and meaning to young people,
> to connect to the civic realities of everyday life and to 'help them
> understand their reality and give them a stake in the future that
> rightly belongs to them.' (citing Kennedy, 1997, p. 3)

Drawing on the US educator Diana Hess's (2009) work, three attributes are also inherent in our use of 'issues' in this chapter. Controversial issues are:

- open and unresolved questions—*really* matters of debate

- authentic—affecting real people in real contexts

- contemporary—issues confronting people, communities and societies today, though the content of such issues is very often a matter of longstanding philosophical and political debate.

Issues education in New Zealand's social studies curricula and classrooms

In this section we consider the expression of issues education in successive New Zealand social studies curricula and, more recently, classrooms. The established international social studies tradition of issues education provides a backdrop for over 50 years of New Zealand social studies engagement with issues. Social studies policy developments (Ministry of Education, 1993, 1997, 2007, 2008) have shaped a social inquiry methodology that embeds a shift to conceptual, critical and reflective inquiry that strongly supports issues education.

While New Zealand social studies educators have long advocated for the inclusion of issues in the curriculum, the presence of issues-based approaches has not been consistently sustained. The curricular acknowledgement of issues education began with *Syllabuses for Schools: Social Studies in the Primary School* (Ministry of Education, 1961) and a set of handbooks[1] (Department of Education, 1971), which had a striking emphasis on "social problems". Students were, for example, expected to evaluate differing ideas, appreciate viewpoints other than their own (Department of Education, 1961) and discover others' beliefs about the good life (Department of Education, 1971). The 1961 document marked the inception of a trend towards values analysis in descriptions of the purposes of social studies education[2] (Aitken, 2005a) and therefore a growing sense of a contested social world. The language of societal complexity, conflict and challenge infused the social studies curriculum and support documents right through to the 1990s, although it was not always a feature of the aims of social studies education.

Aitken (2006) notes that the redrafting of New Zealand's curriculum in 2006 gave "the idea of critical engagement with societal issues more prominence than was the case with the 1997 curriculum" (p. 19). This was achieved through an opening sentence about the purposes of the social sciences learning area, which clearly emphasised students' engagement with societal issues (Ministry of Education, 2006). However, in the learning area's final and current form, the phrase "engage critically with social issues" is embedded some way down the text (Ministry of Education, 2007, p. 30). There is also a noticeable decline in terms that convey societal issues and controversy when compared to its 1997 predecessor, even allowing for marked differences in

---

1 *Suggestions for Teaching Social Studies in the Primary School*, published in 1962, was later reprinted with minor alterations as one book (Department of Education, 1971).
2 Expressed in four New Zealand curriculum documents (Department of Education, 1944, 1977; Ministry of Education, 1961, 1997).

word length (Milligan, 2014). Furthermore, the 2007 curriculum has been criticised for an inadequate sense of conflict, a neutral approach to human agency, and timidity; that is, a refusal to confront the big issues of the day such as global power relationships, conflict and climate change (Hunter, 2007; Snook, 2007).

Perhaps in an effort to reassert the importance of learners' critical engagement with societal controversy, the term 'social issues' is a much greater feature of a subsequent support document, *Building Conceptual Understandings in the Social Sciences: Approaches to Social Inquiry* booklet (Ministry of Education, 2008). This document, and others in the series, supports the exploration of contested issues—such as resource management, globalisation, and remembrance—through a social inquiry approach.

Given that issues are central to the purposes of social studies and citizenship education, how is issues education expressed in New Zealand classrooms? Some insight can be gained from the *International Civic and Citizenship Education Study* (ICCS) (Schulz, Ainley, Fraillon, Kerr, & Losito, 2010), the largest international study on civic and citizenship education ever conducted, in which over 4,000 New Zealand Year 10 students and teachers participated. This revealed that New Zealand students' perceptions of openness in classroom discussions were one of the highest rates for any country that participated in the ICCS. Further insight is offered from a 2011 study (Milligan, Wood, & Taylor, 2013), which sought to investigate how critical thinking about, and responses to, controversial issues are encouraged in social studies classrooms. A total of 872 Year 9 and 10 students, and 39 teachers in 24 schools, responded to a survey. When asked what the best thing was about discussing controversial issues, the majority of students felt it enabled them to understand the issue more clearly and that their voices were being heard (see Figure 3.1). The teachers reported that such discussions enabled students to understand different perspectives, meaning 'angles' on an issue (Figure 3.2). Students were less clear about *how* the teachers enabled them to understand controversial issues, mostly reporting "not sure" (34 percent), "teacher explanations" (35 percent), or presenting "different points of view and opinions" (9 percent).

Figure 3.1: What's the best thing about discussing controversial issues? (Milligan, Wood, & Taylor, 2013)

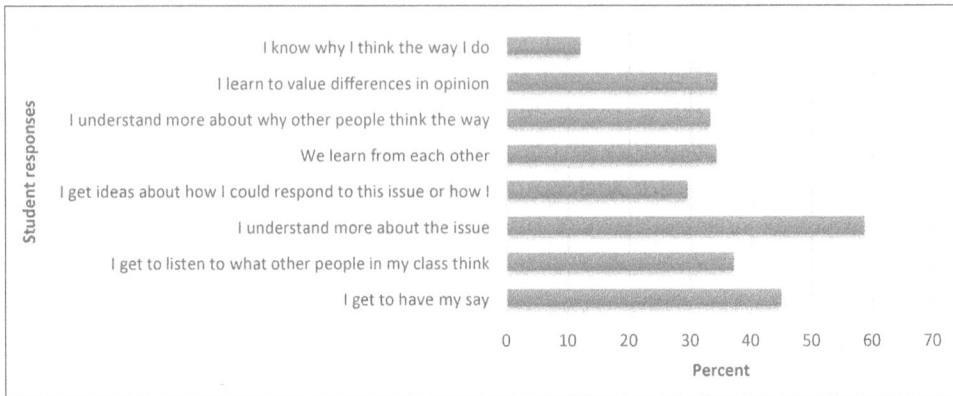

Figure 3.2: What's the best thing about your students discussing controversial issues? (Milligan, Wood, & Taylor, 2013)

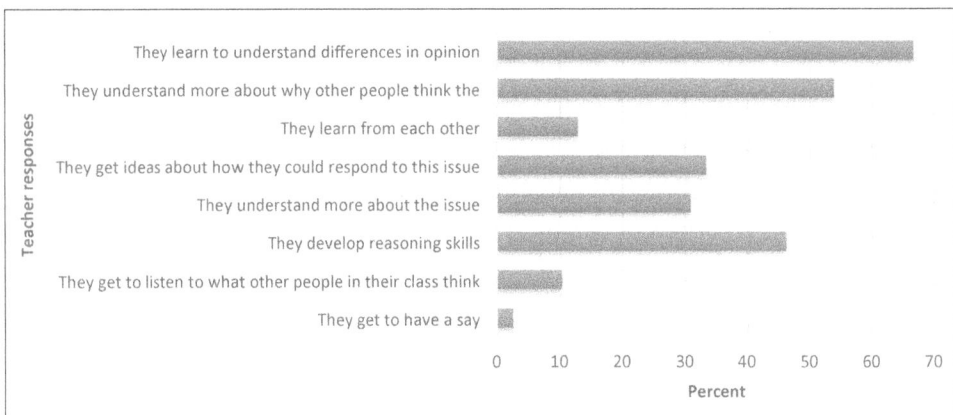

The students' detail about their teachers' pedagogy revealed two key themes. First, the students were often impressed with the length to which their teacher would go to clarify and explain an issue in an unbiased manner. This instilled a sense of confidence in the students that they were getting to the "truth" of the matter:

> She tells us a lot about all issues, she tells us her thoughts and what really happened or [is] happening. She explains in detail because she loves social studies. She helps us get the right idea about it, and makes us think about it. (Student, School 2)

Second, the students typically perceived the exploration of different opinions and points of view as 'two sides' of the story. One student, for example, stated that the teacher showed them "both parts of the story, and get us to do perspective writing. This helps us understand why it is a controversial issue, and look at it from another point of view" (Student, School 26). Taking both these themes together suggests a need for supporting greater nuance in students' conceptions of issues. This is because issues rarely involve simple binaries in people's positions, such as agree/disagree, and the truth can be difficult to arrive at. People's reasoning, values, motivations and commitments are most often complex and, at times, inconsistent. In the next section we consider how this could be achieved through issues-based social inquiry to support citizenship education.

Social inquiry: A methodology for issues-based learning

Chapter 1 introduced social inquiry as a strongly advocated methodology for the Social Sciences learning area, and social studies across Years 1–13. Numerous other models exist internationally for issues-based citizenship education, such as "critical affiliation" (Hill, 1994), "jurisprudential" (Oliver & Shaver, 1986), "decision-making" (Ochoa-Becker, 2007), and "action research" (Gordon, 2000) approaches. While social inquiry shares some of the features of these approaches, it is unique to the New Zealand curriculum and has been developed over successive social studies curriculum documents. A previous iteration, *Social Studies in the New Zealand Curriculum* (Ministry of Education, 1997), identified three inter-related skills processes as being central to learners' understanding about, and participation in, society: inquiry, values exploration and social decision-making, each of which had a reflective and evaluative component. The most recent curriculum and a key support document, *Approaches to Social Inquiry* (Ministry of Education, 2008), have merged these processes into a single "integrated process for examining social issues, ideas, and themes" (p. 5). This comprises the skills processes of:

• questioning and information gathering (inquiry)

• exploring values and perspectives

- considering responses and decision-making
- reflection and evaluation (Ministry of Education, 2007, 2008; Wood, 2013).

The present social inquiry methodology also emphasises the conceptual focus for learning and strengthens the personal and social significance (So what?) and enacted dimensions (Now what?) of the students' investigations. Classroom expressions of social inquiry may incorporate some or all of these skills processes, or they may be shaped by the disciplinary preferences and conventions of, for example, history, geography and economics.

Approaches to Social Inquiry presents a planning framework designed for teacher and student needs (p. 6). In this model, social inquiry stems from the knowledge and conceptual dimension of social studies via selected curriculum achievement objective/s, identification of concepts and ideas, and the defining of a specific context (focus) for inquiry. Establishing an effective inquiry question is important for generating interest and socially critical understanding (Hoepper & McDonald, 2004; Wood, 2013). In the following example the teacher has contextualised a Level 1 achievement objective as a social inquiry question:

- Achievement objective: Understand how belonging to groups is important to people.
- Social inquiry question: How should we help new students feel that they belong to Room Two? Why?

The social inquiry question has a strong conceptual focus on belonging, drawn directly from the achievement objective. Further, the inclusion of the evaluative term 'should' introduces contestability and socially critical understanding by providing scope for exploring values and perspectives, and considering decisions and responses. The question, therefore, embeds both informational goals and transformational/citizenship goals (Wood, 2013).

Hess (2009) suggests that while specific issues are often of interest to students, it can be helpful to identify the links between such "case issues" and wider, perennial debates. This is particularly important given that many students often struggle to see the connectedness across case issues that have been selected by the teacher. Hess contends that "especially powerful learning can occur when teachers are able to help students move inductively and deductively between cases and the perennial issues they exemplify" (p. 43). The key concepts of the curriculum achievement objectives are entry points to both case and perennial social inquiry questions. So, for example, the Level 2 achievement objective about the interaction between people and places may generate questions about specific environmental challenges and more philosophical questions about our obligations to this Earth.

Social inquiry is not the same as generic inquiries, an array of which are employed particularly in primary schools, largely because it draws from the concepts and methodologies of social sciences and humanities disciplines (Mutch, Hunter, Milligan, Openshaw, & Siteine, 2009). One key distinction is that social inquiry has a strong emphasis on the critical exploration and analysis of values and perspectives. Also, and because participatory citizenship lies at the heart of the purposes of social studies, learners are encouraged to take action to bring about social change. Taking action is different from generic inquiries that culminate in sharing information (through, for example, performances, slideshows, displays, or web pages), although these may be useful avenues through which learners are able to press for change.

However, a school's preferred inquiry model does not preclude a social inquiry approach. Table 3.1 identifies some of the connections between one school's iCycle model and social inquiry (Ministry of Education, 2007, 2008). The connections identified are indicative rather than exhaustive, and it is also important to note that the rather linear nature of the table belies the reiterative nature of social inquiry and the iCycle model.

An issues-based social inquiry is likely to present an opportunity for integrating concepts and conceptual understandings within an authentic context. Why does this matter? Selected contexts may evoke empathy and emotions, and may relate to something in the community that students would like to understand better, or to change. Michael Harcourt's vignette "Teaching Controversy and the Treaty of Waitangi" (see p. 51), illustrates this point. Initially his approach to teaching this wasn't going very well. After seeking student feedback, he realised that there was no real controversy embedded in the learning and that it wasn't sufficiently

Table 3.1: Connections between social inquiry and a generic iCycle inquiry model

NZC	Approached to social inquiry	iCycle inquiry
Ask questions, gather information and background ideas, and examine relevant **current issues**	Establishing the focus for learning Finding out information	Wondering Knowledge Comprehension
Explore and analyse people's values and perspectives	Exploring values and perspectives	Analysis
Consider the ways in which people make decisions and participate in social action	Considering decisions and responses	Analysis
	Now what? Taking action Next learning steps	Application
Reflect on and evaluate the understandings that have developed the responses that may be required	So what? What do we know now? Significance for us/others?	Synthesis
	Reflecting and evaluating	Evaluation

Source for iCycle model: http://intranet.kings.school.nz/students/pages/icycle.html

connected to the present. So he provided them with a contemporary scenario: the replacement of Waitangi Day with New Zealand Day. The promotion of controversy engaged a previously difficult class, developed their critical thinking skills, and enabled them to see how the historical antecedents of an issue connect with, and continue in, the present. The Year 10 students' misconceptions were challenged by critically focused, creative information gathering and processing activity, in which they explored perspectives (as broad values systems, or world views) and debated the proposal from the position of their allocated perspective. Michael's approach shifted from countering misconceptions by providing information, to a social inquiry approach (aspects of which are highlighted to the right of the vignette) that encouraged students to wrestle with the contested nature of perspectives and decision making.

Teaching controversy and the Treaty of Waitangi

Teaching the Treaty of Waitangi in my school often generates complaints and resistance from students. In a recent Year 10 class my initial response was to try and engage the class by challenging their misconceptions. Wearing my history teacher's hat, I attempted to develop students' understanding of multiple perspectives at the time of the signing: who signed, and why, as well as who didn't and the reasons for that. I was particularly interested in highlighting that the Treaty was not signed in the wake of a war between Māori and Pākehā, which many believed.

However, there was still too much resistance for the learning to gain momentum. I decided to redesign the unit in ways that more deliberately explored the controversy associated with the Treaty in New Zealand today and in students' own lives. The task I developed was to script and perform the first reading of a parliamentary debate about an imaginary new law abolishing Waitangi Day and replacing it with 'New Zealand Day'. The reason given for this law change was that Waitangi Day had become too divisive and New Zealanders needed something more unifying to celebrate as their national day. **To prepare, we explored what they thought about the idea of the Bill, visited Parliament and learned about law changes and parliamentary debates.** We also watched clips of historical New Zealand parliamentary debates, noting the tone and language used by politicians. Finally, students were put into groups that represented un-named political parties for either the government or the opposition. In their groups students were allocated perspectives, or broad values systems, that shape how people might respond to the issue of replacing Waitangi Day with New Zealand Day.

    The perspectives were *biculturalism, multiculturalism* and *nationalism*. Students were given a handout which outlined some key assumptions of each perspective. These included "The Crown has particular obligations to Māori as the indigenous people of New Zealand and the Crown's Treaty partner" (biculturalism), New Zealand is a multicultural society that should officially recognise the cultures of many different peoples" (multiculturalism), and "sameness or unity needs to be actively promoted by the government so that people identify to their nation" (a nationalist perspective). **Students had to argue their position, writing and performing their speech for the First Reading of the Bill from their allocated perspective**. The debate was videoed and presented at a learning exhibition for parents. Highlighting the contested and contemporary nature of the topic meant that I was able to engage my reluctant Year 10 class in thinking critically about the Treaty of Waitangi and its role in New Zealand society.

Margin notes:
- Finding out information
- Exploring values and perspectives
- Considering decisions and responses

Michael's vignette illustrates what an observant, informed and motivated teacher can do to immerse Year 10 students in an issue that has historical, contemporary and future resonances. The authentic, issue-based context and social inquiry approach engaged his students in public concerns that had personal connections (Hess & Posselt, 2002). Moreover, he conceived of his students as "thinking individuals deserving of respect" (Ochoa-Becker, 2007, p. 100); that is, as *already* citizens (Biesta, 2011).

Exploring the nuances and complexities of issues through social inquiry

Social dilemmas, contestation, controversy and competing ideologies (Banks & Nguyen, 2008) are the stuff of issues-based social inquiry. This is because, to return to the opening section of this chapter, facts and information alone are insufficient for supporting students to explore the profoundly contentious, ethical dimensions of participating in society. Each process skill of social inquiry enables a critical consideration of nuance and complexity. For example, *exploring values and perspectives* challenges students in emotional and intellectual ways because they may be exposed to divergent rather than normative views, particularly when dealing with differing viewpoints, diversity, and cultural and gendered representations (Keown, 1998; Ministry of Education, 1997; Wendt-Samu, 2004). *Considering responses and decision making* engages students in dialogue and debate about different visions for social action and transformation, which may give rise to dealing with tensions, problem-solving, and seeking resolution. This promotes critical thinking for multiple solutions, healthy scepticism, and attention to tensions between, for example, freedom and social control, unity and diversity (Westheimer & Kahne, 2003). *Reflection and evaluation* reinforces the essentially provisional nature of visions for change; that is, that ideas are always open to further scrutiny. It enables students to consider the contested and often taken-for-granted nature of concepts that people use when deliberating about issues (Milligan & Wood, 2010) and the culturally located and contextual nature of knowledge.

The sociocultural and constructivist thinking (Barr, 2005; McNeil, 2006; Scheurman, 1998) that encourages student-led social inquiry means that teachers' pedagogical and content decision-making have never been more important. So how can teachers get the most out of issues-based social inquiry? Although there is not the space here to offer a textbook of instructional strategies, this section indicates some practical considerations for enabling students to explore the nuances of societal issues.

(i) Procedure

The importance of clear structures for issues-based learning cannot be overstated, in part because this goes a long way towards managing the dynamics of controversy in the classroom. The syntactical or procedural knowledge of social inquiry provides a *method* (a way of doing) for exploring issues, and a *lens* (a way of seeing or knowing) through which learners can consider the complexities and nuances of such issues, which is informed by disciplinary perspectives. For an issues-based context, social inquiry can be developed as a learning cycle through all skills processes, and it is important that all learners be able to 'see the whole'. However, social inquiry is dependent on students' interests, maturity, prior experiences, knowledge, and the nature of the selected context. This means that an entry point into social inquiry could be, for example, exploring values and perspectives, or considering decisions and responses (as with Michael's vignette), or reflecting and evaluating, to initiate a partial or whole cycle of social inquiry.

Investing in teaching students to identify and apply the distinct skills processes of social inquiry means they are made aware of the functions and possibilities of each process skill and develop greater sophistication in their understandings of issues. A wide range of strategies is available to support social inquiry procedures and process skill development (see Chapters 4 and 5; Keown, 1998, 1999; Ministry of Education, 2008). Importantly, teachers need to evaluate the extent to which each strategy fosters appreciation for the complexities of the issue in focus, and resists simplistic pro/con, for/against, right/wrong thinking. Hilary Claire (2003) notes, for example, that

> The conventional techniques of dividing groups up to represent
> different perspectives and then share these, can actually work
> to reinforce specific positions rather than move towards mutual
> understanding and open mindedness. It may be more important to
> get students to mount a rational argument for the opposing position

to their own, or to set out all perspectives of an argument. (p. 19)

In almost all cases, a range of strategies is needed to build social inquiry process skills and expand students' insight into an issue. For example, Michael's students' understanding of different perspectives could be strengthened by the structured academic controversy method,[3] in which students take up alternative positions in order to reach an enlarged understanding of the issue, rather than 'winning the argument'. The important point is *how* strategies are used to generate nuanced thinking. For example, values continua, a commonly used strategy for values exploration, can be used simplistically for sharing opinions and viewpoints. A richer approach might involve students examining the commonalities that exist between seemingly extreme positions, or how the same value is interpreted differently.

(ii) Preparation

Challenging assumptions and developing a sufficient depth of understanding about an issue require careful preparation on the part of teachers and students. Part of teachers' preparation involves their own self-reflection. Just as family, life experiences and media socialise young people and shape their knowledge and skills, teachers can limit or positively affect students' engagement with challenging issues and difficult knowledge. A teacher's personal views, preferences and assumptions are likely to influence the nature of the issues explored. Denial of teacher privilege (Hess, 2004), the avoidance of controversy, a lack of open-minded engagement with divergent perspectives, or unwillingness to counter students' misconceptions undermines issues-based social studies. Moreover, teachers need to be alert to silences created by a hidden or unintended curriculum that reflects dominant discourses; for example, the absence of Māori and Pākehā concepts that relate to injustice and power relationships in the Social Sciences learning area (Ministry of Education, 2007).

In short, teachers' mindfulness about their content knowledge for social inquiry and pedagogy for issues-based learning is central to their students' understanding of nuance and complexity. Another essential element of teacher preparation is identifying suitable texts to support social inquiry. Very often this information-gathering

---

3   http://teachinghistory.org/teaching-materials/teaching-guides/21731

phase is an opportune time to teach the skills of accessing and assessing sources. However, when other aspects of social inquiry, such as exploring values and perspectives, are the focus for learning, teachers may justifiably elect to provide the source materials. It is at this point that the complexity of an issue can be illuminated—and silences addressed—through the careful selection of open-ended texts that demand more than comprehension. By this we mean visual, oral and written texts that:

• allow varied interpretations, such as a story, artwork or image
• offer more than two angles on an issue; that is, the perspectives of a range of people and groups on an issue or idea
• include conflicting evidence about the causes of an issue and/or possible responses
• provide opportunities to explore inferences and assumptions.

The richest learning usually stems from selecting texts that are in dialogue with each other; that is, a combination of texts that reveal an unresolved conversation or debate about an issue. Social studies students need support to decode and make meaning from such texts, and it cannot be overstated that supportive literacy strategies[4] need to be factored into the preparation process.

Great issues-based social inquiry may sit within planned-for programme delivery or it may depart from a topic's framing to seize the immediacy of issues alive in the public eye. However, at all times preparation is essential, and Michael's vignette gives an insight into just how much preparation is required for classroom debate so that students understand the subtleties involved. Hess (2002) stresses that off-the-cuff discussions rarely result in robust understanding of an issue. One strategy she advocates is 'student tickets', in which students come to class having prepared a report about an issue as a way to ensure they have sufficient content knowledge to enter into a debate. Students who have not prepared their 'ticket' instead become observers of the discussion, and provide feedback about the quality of the discussion to others in their class.

---

4   See http://www.literacyonline.tki.org.nz

(iii) Positions

Promoting nuanced understanding of issues involves being well informed about societal issues as a teacher, observing students' conceptual understanding and skills development, and engaging students in dialogue to find out about their affective responses, such as receptivity or resistance, to an issue. Managing the potential heat and uncertainty involved adds another layer of challenge. This requires secure classroom cultures where trust, respect and purposeful inquiry support students to experience democracy in action. Claire (2003) suggests that creating an atmosphere of open-minded social inquiry involves enabling students to:

- recognise the variety of values positions and concepts that people are drawing on
- develop critical thinking skills, such as providing logical, convincing arguments that draw on evidence, and recognising how arguments can be manipulated
- develop interpersonal skills, such as respectfulness, diplomacy, tact and trust.

While a completely values-free approach is unlikely to be possible, teachers who are aware of their own biases, and perhaps fear indoctrination, are often unsure of what role to take. This is particularly the case when class discussions form part of the social inquiry process. Table 3.2 identifies some positions teachers can take, together with the drawbacks of each, drawn from the work of Holden (2007, column 1) and Oxfam (2006, column 2). It is important to note that teachers do not have to permanently align themselves with one approach. Instead, a particular position, or combination thereof, is strategically selected in order to introduce more nuance into students' debates and explorations. Readers might note, for example, that Michael's vignette reflects the deliberate selection of a balanced approach, along with aspects of a neutral chair approach, as outlined below.

Table 3.2: Possibilities for a teacher's role in an issues discussion

Holden (2007)	Oxfam (2006)
The neutral chair. This requires the teacher not to express any personal views, as these may be given undue weight by pupils, but to act only as a facilitator. However, this denies pupils the opportunity to hear the teacher's views and means the teacher cannot model how to give an opinion, backed up by evidence.	*Impartial chairperson.* The teacher ensures that all viewpoints are represented, through pupil statements or published sources. The teacher facilitates but refrains from stating his/her own position.
The balanced approach. In this teachers ensure that all aspects of an issue are covered. The teacher expresses his/her view in order to encourage the students to present theirs. The teacher ensures that a range of opinions are expressed. This approach can run the risk of giving equal weight to all arguments and leaving students confused as to those of real merit.	*Objective or academic.* The teacher transmits an explanation of all possible viewpoints without stating his/her own position. *Advocate.* The teacher presents all available viewpoints, then concludes by stating his/her own position with reasons. The teacher can then make the point that it is important for pupils to evaluate all viewpoints before forming their own opinions.
Stated commitment approach. The teacher openly expresses his/her view as a means of encouraging discussion, but it can run the risk of indoctrinating students.	*Committed.* The teacher is free to propagate his/her own views. Care needs to be taken with this role, however, as this can lead to a biased discussion. *Declared interest.* The teacher declares his/her own viewpoint so that pupils can judge later bias, then presents all available positions as objectively as possible.
Challenging consensus approach. In this the teacher consciously and openly takes up an opposite position to that expressed by participants or resource material in order to challenge the prevailing viewpoints.	*Devil's advocate.* The teacher adopts provocative and oppositional stances irrespective of his/her own viewpoint. This enables the teacher to ensure that all views are covered and challenged if a consensus view emerges early on. It also helps to challenge young people's existing beliefs.

Conclusion: Issues-based social inquiry and the centre of citizenship education

Issues-based social inquiry has been unpacked in this chapter to illustrate its currency and purpose in social learning. The chapter began with a reflection on the 'business' of social studies in terms of young people's understanding of social worlds and their active and ethical participation within these worlds. Social studies must enable young people to navigate the social worlds they live in and move across, in an age of migration, diversity and redefining of social boundaries.

At least three concepts have framed the chapter's issues-based social inquiry and citizenship education focus: *uncertainty, controversy* and *visions of change*. A proactive, relevant social studies programme must surely reflect society's current controversies, unresolved issues and differing visions of change and social reconstruction (McNeil, 2006). Ultimately our goal is "to encourage respect for perspective, uncertainty, and provisionality as preparation for living in an increasingly pluralistic, fragmented, and rapidly changing world" (Skelton, 1997, p.187).

Issues-based social inquiry is not simply a procedure. Taught well, it is democratic citizenship *in practice* because it presents an entry point for students' own deliberations about critical, active and ethical participation in society. An issues-based approach to social studies and citizenship education holds the potential to support a nuanced understanding of society and social participation, enabling them to see, for example, how world views and decision-making processes play out differently across community settings. Such an approach goes well beyond the more traditional 'inquiry' exercise of findings and sorting 'the facts', and instead engages students directly with navigating the controversial dimensions of their social worlds. Accordingly, teachers, educators and researchers need to assert issues-based social inquiry's central role in supporting young citizens' social participation.

Reflective questions

- To what extent do your social studies programmes meet the criteria of an 'issue', as established by Aitken and Hess?

- How might designing issues-based programmes support the teaching of *perspectives* as outlined in Chapter 4?

- To what extent do your programmes allow student voice in selecting issues that are relevant to them? What challenges and opportunities does giving students more voice in selecting issues present to teachers?

- How might your school's local area, its community resources and any challenges it faces be used as a springboard for designing an issues-based social studies programme?

References

Aitken, G. (2005a). *Curriculum design in New Zealand social studies: Learning from the past.* Unpublished doctoral thesis, University of Auckland.

Aitken, G. (2005b). The purpose and substance of social studies: Citizenship education possibilities. In P. Benson & R. Openshaw (Eds.), *Towards effective social studies* (pp. 85–112). Palmerston North: Kanuka Grove Press.

Aitken, G. (2006). Signalling shifts in meaning: The experience of social studies curriculum design. *Curriculum Matters, 2,* 6–25.

Banks, J., & Nguyen, D. (2008). Diversity and citizenship education: Historical, theoretical, and philosophical issues. In L. Levstik & C. Tyson (Eds.), *Handbook of research in social studies education* (pp. 137–151). New York, NY: Routledge.

Barr, H. (1998). The nature of social studies. In P. Benson & R. Openshaw (Eds.), *New horizons for New Zealand social studies* (pp. 103–120). Palmerston North: ERDC Press.

Barr, H. (2005). The fourth C: Constructivism. *New Zealand Journal of Social Studies, 13,* 5–7.

Barr, H., Graham, J., Hunter, P., Keown, P., & McGee, J. (1997). *A position paper: Social studies in the New Zealand school curriculum.* Hamilton: University of Waikato.

Biesta, G. (2011). *Learning democracy in school and society: Education, learning and the politics of citizenship.* Rotterdam, The Netherlands: Sense Publishers.

Carrington, B., & Troyna, B. (1988). *Children and controversial issues: Strategies for the early and middle years of schooling.* London, UK: Falmer.

Claire, H. (2003). Dealing with controversial issues with primary teacher trainees as part of citizenship education. *citizED.* Retrieved from http://www.citized.info/?strand=0&r_menu=res

Claire, H., & Holden, C. (Eds.). (2007). *The challenge of teaching controversial issues.* Staffordshire, UK: Trentham Books.

Dearden, R. F. (1981). Controversial issues and the curriculum. *Journal of Curriculum Studies, 13*(1), 37–44. doi:10.1080/0022027810130105

Department of Education. (1971). *Suggestions for teaching social studies in the primary school: Parts I, II, III, IV.* Wellington: Government Printer.

Department of Education. (1961). *Syllabuses for schools: Social studies in the primary school.* Wellington: Author.

Evans, R. W., & Saxe, D. W. (Eds.). (1996). *Handbook on teaching social issues: NCSS bulletin 93.* Washington, DC: National Council for the Social Studies

Gilbert, R., & Hoepper, B. (Eds.). (2004). *Teaching society and the environment* (4th ed.). South Melbourne, VIC: Cengage Learning.

Gordon, K. (2000). *Inquiry approaches in the primary studies of society and environment key learning area.* Retrieved from www.qsa.qld.edu.au/downloads/.../research_qscc_sose_primary_00.doc.

Hess, D. E. (2002). Discussing controversial public issues in secondary social studies classrooms: Learning from skilled teachers. *Theory & Research in Social Education, 30*(1), 10–41. doi: 10.1080/00933104.2002.10473177.

Hess, D. (2004). Controversies about controversial issues in democratic education. *Political Science and Politics, 37*(2), 257–261. doi: org/10.1017/S1049096504004196.

Hess, D. (2008). Controversial issues and democratic discourse. In L. S. Levstik & C. A. Tyson (Eds.), *Handbook of research in social studies education* (pp. 124–136). New York, NY: Routledge.

Hess, D. (2009). *Controversy in the classroom: The democratic power of discussion.* London, UK: Routledge.

Hess, D., & Posselt, J. (2002). How high school students experience and learn from the discussion of controversial public issues. *Journal of Curriculum and Supervision, 17*(4), 283–314.

Hill, B. V. (1994). *Teaching secondary social studies in a multicultural society.* Melbourne, VIC: Longman Cheshire.

Hoepper, B., & McDonald, H. (2004). Critical inquiry in SOSE: The big picture. In R. Gilbert (Ed.), *Studying society and environment: A guide for teachers* (pp. 22–36). Southbank, VIC: Thomson.

Holden, C. (2007). Controversy for beginners: How to keep calm and maintain control while teaching about controversial issues. *citizED.* http://www.citized.info/?strand=0&r_menu=res

Hunter, P. (2007). Comment: Social sciences in the New Zealand curriculum: A case of arrested development? Mediating challenges ahead. *Teachers and Curriculum, 10,* 47–50.

Kennedy, K. (Ed.). (1997). *Citizenship education and the modern state.* London, UK: Falmer.

Keown, P. (1998). Values and social action: Doing the hard bits. In P. Benson & R. Openshaw (Eds.), *New horizons for New Zealand social studies.* Palmerston North: ERDC Press.

Keown, P. (1999). Some strategies for the development of the values exploration and social decision making processes. *Social Studies on Broadway: Proceedings of the 1999 FSSA Conference*. Palmerston North: Federation of Social Studies Associations of New Zealand.

Levinson, R. (2006). Towards a theoretical framework for teaching controversial socio-scientific Issues. *International Journal of Science Education, 28*(10), 1201–1224. doi: 10.1080/09500690600560753.

McNeil, J. D. (2006). *Contemporary curriculum in thought and action* (6th ed.). Hoboken, NJ: John Wiley & Sons.

Milligan, A. (2014). *Transcending the ethically silent space of the New Zealand social studies curriculum*. Unpublished doctoral thesis, Victoria University of Wellington.

Milligan, A., & Wood, B. E. (2010). Conceptual understandings as transition points: Making sense of a complex social world. *Journal of Curriculum Studies, 42*(4), 487–501. doi: 10.1080/00220270903494287.

Milligan, A., Wood, B. E., & Taylor, M. A. (2013, July). *Teaching critical thinking about controversial issues in social studies*. Paper presented at the Social Sciences Conference Aotearoa New Zealand, Hamilton.

Ministry of Education. (1993). *The New Zealand curriculum framework*. Wellington: Learning Media.

Ministry of Education. (1997). *Social studies in the New Zealand curriculum*. Wellington: Learning Media.

Ministry of Education. (2006). *The New Zealand curriculum: Draft for consultation*. Wellington: Learning Media.

Ministry of Education. (2007). *The New Zealand curriculum*. Wellington: Learning Media.

Ministry of Education. (2008). *Building conceptual understandings in the social sciences: Approaches to social inquiry*. Wellington: Learning Media.

Mutch, C., Hunter, P., Milligan, A., Openshaw, R., & A. Siteine. (2009). *Understanding the social sciences as a learning area: A position paper*. Retrieved from http://nzcurriculum.tki.org.nz/curriculum-resources/nzc-resource. bank/social.sciences/key-resources.

Nelson, J. (1996). The historical imperative for issues-centred education. In R. W. Evans & D. W. Saxe (Eds.), *Handbook on teaching social issues: NCSS Bulletin 93* (pp. 14–24). Washington, DC: National Council for the Social Studies.

Ochoa-Becker, A. (2007). Socialization and counter socialization for a democracy. *Democratic education for social studies: An issues-centered decision making curriculum*. New York, NY: Information Age Publishing.

Oliver, D., & Shaver, J. P. (1986). *Teaching public issues in the high school*. Boston, MA: Houghton Mifflin.

Oulton, C., Day, V., Dillon, J., & Grace, M. (2004). Controversial issues: Teachers' attitudes and practices in the context of citizenship education. *Oxford Review of Education, 30*(4), 489–507. doi: 10.1080/0305498042000303973.

Oxfam (2006). *Global citizenship guides: Teaching controversial issues*. Retrieved from http://www.oxfam.org.uk/education/teachersupport/cpd/controversial/files/teaching_controversial_issues.pdf .

Patrick, J. J., Vontz, T. S., & Nixon, W. A. (2002). Issues-centred education for democracy through Project Citizen. In W. C. Parker (Ed.), *Education for democracy: Contexts, curricula and assessments* (pp. 93–112). Greenwich, CT: Information Age.

Reynolds, R. (2009). *Teaching studies of society and the environment*. South Melbourne, VIC: Oxford University Press.

Ross, E. W. (2006). *The social studies curriculum: Purposes, problems, and possibilities* (3rd ed.). New York, NY: State University of New York.

Saxe, D. W. (1992). Framing a theory for social studies foundations. *Review of Educational Research, 62*(3), 259–277. doi: 10.2307/1170739

Scheurman, G. (1998). From behaviourist to constructive teaching. *Social Education, 62*(1), 6–9.

Schulz, W., Ainley, J., Fraillon, J., Kerr, D., & Losito, B. (2010). *ICCS 2009: Civic knowledge, attitudes, and engagement among lower secondary school students in 38 countries*. Amsterdam, The Netherlands: IEA.

Shaver, J. P. (1992). Rationales for issues-centred social studies education. *Social Studies, 83*(3), 95–100.

Skelton, A. (1997). Studying hidden curricula: Developing a perspective in the light of postmodern insights. *Curriculum Studies, 5*(2), 177–193.

Snook, I. (2007). The timid curriculum. *Teachers and Curriculum, 10*, 39–42.

Stenhouse, L. (1971). The humanities curriculum project: The rationale. *Theory into Practice, 10*(3), 154–162. doi: org/10.1080/00405847109542322.

Stradling, R. (1984). The teaching of controversial issues: An evaluation. *Educational Review, 36*(2), 121–129. doi: 10.1080/0013191840360202.

Wellington, J. J. (Ed.). (1986). *Controversial issues in the classroom*. Oxford, UK: Basil Blackwell.

Wendt-Samu, T. (2004). Multiple lenses, multiple ways of seeing our world: Some critical reflections. *New Zealand Journal of Social Studies, 12*(1), 8–13.

Westheimer, J., & Kahne, J. (2003). Reconnecting education to democracy: Democratic dialogues. *Phi Delta Kappan, 85*(1), 9–14.

Wood, B. E. (2013). What is a social inquiry? Crafting questions that lead to deeper knowledge about society and citizenship. *set: Research Information for Teachers, 3*, 20–28.

Chapter 4 Deepening thinking through viewpoints, values and perspectives

Mike Taylor and Paul Keown

Key points

- Exploring viewpoints, values and perspectives is fundamental to social inquiry.
- In social studies teaching and learning, viewpoints, values and perspectives are related but not synonymous ideas.
- Viewpoints, values and perspectives are tools to help students develop their competence to think critically.

Introduction

Chapter 3 introduced the idea that social studies education recognises that people inevitably see the world differently. Sociocultural factors such as place of origin, gender, ethnicity, political leaning, age and previous experiences are some of the influences on how people see their world. Contemporary questions such as 'How should New Zealand respond to global environmental pressures?', 'Should we accept the predominant ANZAC narrative?' or 'Does technological change equate with progress?' are unsettled because of the differences in viewpoints, values and perspectives that permeate such issues.

Despite teachers knowing that exploring values and perspectives is important, Keown (1998) suggests that this component of social studies education has been commonly sidestepped for a range of philosophical and practical reasons. For example, traditional content-based approaches to teaching subject knowledge have stymied the consideration of contested knowledge, and some teachers have avoided exploring values for fear of being accused of political indoctrination. Keown labels values and perspectives as the "hard bits" of social studies because teachers have also been unsure of the efficacy of strategies to explicitly teach this area of the curriculum.

Empirical studies from New Zealand since Keown's work give little assurance that the hard bits have become easier for teachers of social studies (Education Review Office, 2006; Notman et al., 2012). However, in this chapter we suggest that viewpoints, values and perspectives can be well understood and effectively implemented if they are seen as tools to deepen learners' critical thinking about society. We do this by revisiting these fundamental social studies concepts, which, while related, have very different meanings. Our objectives in this chapter are therefore to:

- clarify the important differences between viewpoints, values and perspectives in order to support issues-based social inquiry
- explore the extent to which values and perspectives continue to be regarded as the 'hard bits'
- offer practical examples of how critical thinking about these terms might be deepened.

Distinguishing between viewpoints, values and perspectives

New Zealand social studies education distinguishes between the terms 'viewpoints', 'values' and 'perspectives' as a way to encourage learners, in age-appropriate ways, to understand different views in, and of, complex and contested societies. Two resources for clarifying the distinctions between these terms, useful for both primary and secondary teachers, are the *Building Conceptual Understanding in the Social Sciences* series (see Ministry of Education, 2008) and the senior social studies teaching and learning guide (Ministry of Education, 2013). These materials present viewpoints, values and perspectives as a nested relationship, in which values and perspectives form an often unstated backdrop to people's points of view. Exploring *all three* components of seeing the world through social inquiry allows students to analyse the way individuals' views are anchored by deeply held beliefs, which are simultaneously part of much broader, collective world views. In the following sections we explore the concepts of viewpoints, values and perspectives in greater depth.

Viewpoints

The concept of viewpoint or 'opinion' is relatively well understood, probably because in ordinary conversation individuals are often asked "What is your view?", meaning "What do you think about this?". A viewpoint has, in relation to the concepts of values and perspectives, a vernacular dimension to it that is located in everyday experience and is readily understood by young students. Thinking about issues in society by exploring viewpoints necessarily requires attention to whether the viewpoints are driven by strong evidence or are shaped by emotion, beliefs and gut feeling. Using an iceberg analogy (see Figure 4.1), opinions, like behaviours, are above the surface and are evident in the public realm. While attitudes can sometimes be masked, opinions and behaviour are clearly visible to those who interact with them or observe them in action in the public sphere.

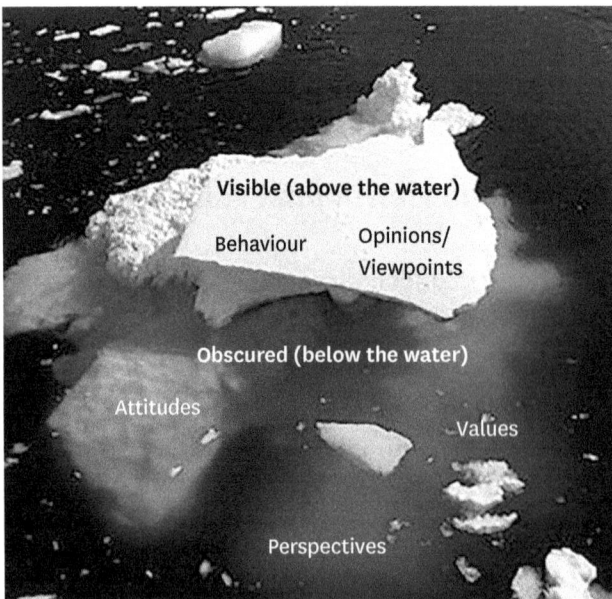

Figure 4.1: Iceberg analogy of viewpoints, values and perspectives (Source Image by Jason Auche, CC BY 2.0)

In some instances people can have widely opposed viewpoints. For example, groups like Greenpeace and the Japanese whaling companies are so far apart that they firmly believe each other is wrong, leading to aggressive tactics to stop one another from whaling or protesting. In most instances, however, people can agree on some aspects of an issue and disagree on others—and it is important that social studies teaching and learning support students to see this kind of subtlety.

Values

At a deeper level of the iceberg, values are "deep", often "private", and can be difficult to change (Keown, Parker, & Tiakiwai, 2005). Rokeach (1973) defines a value as "an enduring belief that a specific mode of conduct or end-states of existence is personally or socially preferable to an opposite or converse mode of conduct or end-states of existence" (p. 5). Such a definition emphasises that values can involve questions about goals (ends) and about how we get to those goals (modes of conduct). This is not to say that we are always clear about our values: sometimes we can be unaware of the values we hold, or find it difficult to articulate them.

In recent years schools are likely to have given careful attention to the list of values highlighted in the front end of *The New Zealand Curriculum* (*NZC*) (Ministry of Education, 2007, p. 10). According to Strike (1999), in order to develop a sense of school community, schools are likely to consider "big-tented values", similar to the 10 currently presented in the *NZC*. Strike describes such values as "thick, but vague": values are pitched in a form that appears so broadly acceptable that it is hard to see who is likely to reject them. Yet such broad values, when placed in context, are rarely unproblematic, especially if these values conflict. This was highlighted by a New Zealand Environment Court judge who criticised Fonterra's discharge of waste from its Edgecumbe plant into the Rangitaiki River as valuing productivity ahead of the environment (Sharpe, 2015). In this example, the failure of an industry leader to practise its own commitment to safeguarding natural resources and reducing its environmental impact (Fonterra, 2014) echoes a contention that "having certain values does not guarantee that we will act in accordance with what we cherish as worthwhile" (Burgh, Field, & Freakley, 2006, p. 44).

It is partly for this reason that the *NZC's Values Statement* (Ministry of Education, 2007) advocates values *analysis* and exploration alongside the encouragement/inculcation of particular values. International advocacy for values analysis was closely tied to the post-World War II development of the social sciences (Chandler, 1979). Proponents argued for the logical, rational analysis of social values (Scriven, 1966), in which an issue is defined and arguments are weighed before arriving at a defensible judgement. This deeper thinking approach to values recognises that social issues are most often the result of competing, colliding and fluid values.

Realising the aim of enabling young people to "engage critically with societal issues" (Ministry of Education, 2007, p. 30) requires curriculum-making that is attuned to contexts in which values-based conflict is centralised. As a fundamental aspect of New Zealand social studies teaching and learning (Taylor & Atkins, 2005), successive curricula have encouraged the exploration of values conflict through analysing, for example, how values positions can change over time, be evaluated by different criteria, and be prioritised by people at different times depending on the context (for further aspects, see Ministry of Education, 1997). In another example, Crompton and Weinstein (2015) draw attention to the mapping of clusters of values that, we believe, could offer social studies teachers and their students a more nuanced way to explore values-based conflict. Based on decades of Schwartz's (2006) cross-cultural social psychology research, this mapping of values (Figure 4.2, below) indicates that clusters in close proximity are more likely to be prioritised at the same time, while those on opposite sides of the map are less likely to be strongly held at the same time.

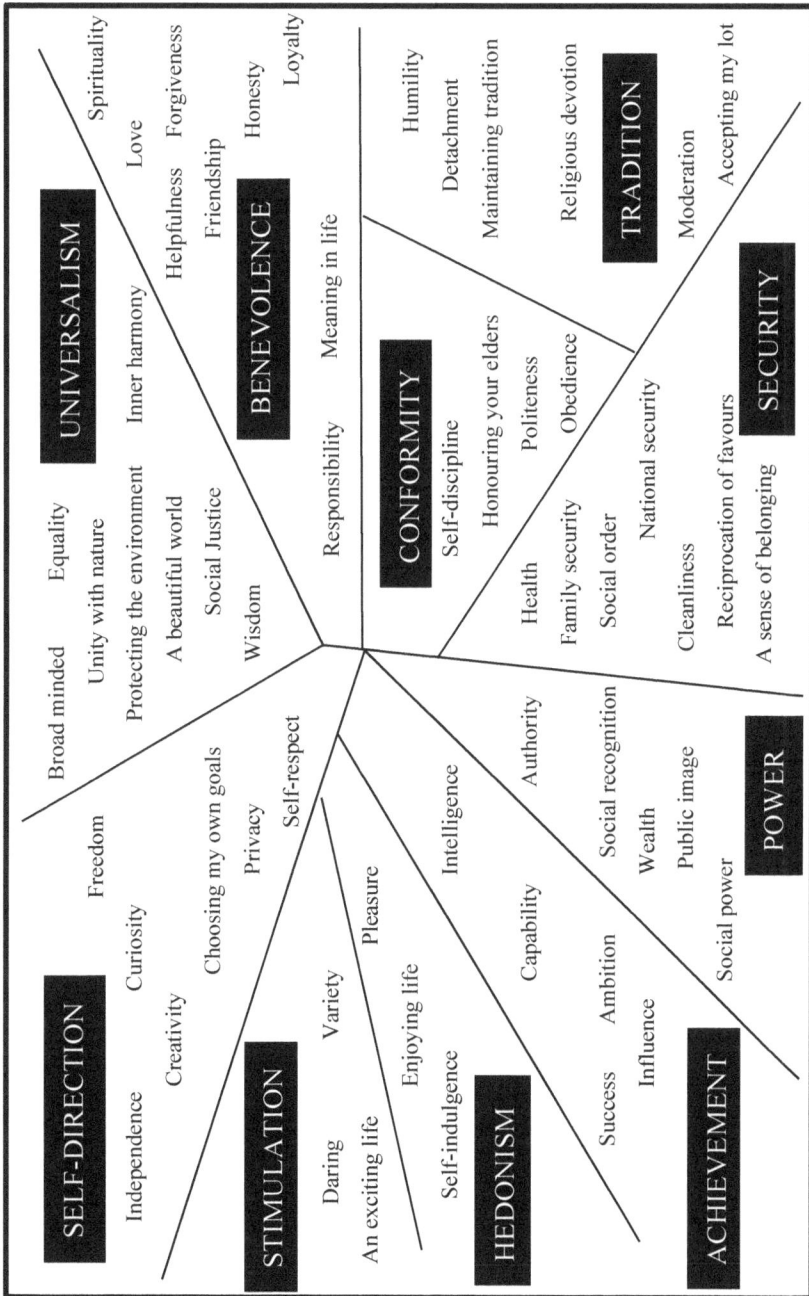

Figure 4.2: A map of basic human values. [Redrawn, with permission, from Schwartz (2006) and Crompton and Weinstein (2015)]

Perspectives

In everyday language the term 'perspective' is used in two main ways: the opinion or beliefs of a particular group on a topic or issue (in this sense it is very similar to 'viewpoint'), or as meaning 'understanding the relative importance of things', as in 'get things in perspective'. The nature of perspectives, as signposted in the senior social studies curriculum support materials, suggests, however, a very different meaning than common usages of the word:

> students develop their understanding of how people's points of view and values are shaped by a complex and intersecting landscape of perspectives. Other words for this are worldviews, ways of looking at the world, lenses, paradigms, ideologies, and theoretical frameworks … It is the complexity and fluidity of people's responses that we want students to understand rather than a static impression of how people and groups operate in society. (Ministry of Education, 2013, n.p.)

The Ministry guidelines for social studies use 'perspectives' in a way that geography teachers are likely to be familiar with. The New Zealand geography educator Frances Slater (1993) called perspectives "ideologies", or "worldviews", describing them as "bundles of beliefs, opinions, attitudes, values and preferences that people hold together. They explain a lot about how people act and behave" (p. 123). The similarity with the Ministry guidelines for social studies is striking. However, when teaching social studies, senior history teachers may have to reorient their usual use of perspective, which is more typically associated with appreciating the experiences and actions of an individual rather than their theoretical orientation.

Social studies perspectives are, not surprisingly, the deepest of the ideas on the iceberg analogy. They are collective world views that have developed over time, are held by many people, and often involve a range of values and beliefs. Senior secondary social studies students are expected to have grasped a nuanced understanding of perspectives. For example, an umbrella term such as 'green' perspectives can involve different levels of emphasis given to environmental change through technological fixes, management approaches through legislation, or social justice and Gaianist reorientations to production and consumption (Stevenson, 1987). This kind of perspectives thinking is an opportunity for teachers and students to think critically about the link between values, decisions and actions; to ask, for example, 'What are the effects of this perspective?', 'Who stands to benefit?' and 'What other ways of thinking are possible?'.

Values and perspectives: still the 'hard bits' of social studies?

International and local studies have shown that though teachers acknowledge the importance of including the study of values and perspectives in classroom units of work, they are uncertain about how to work with values and perspectives in a classroom context (Keown, 1998; Powney et al., 1995; Stevenson, Ling, Burman, & Cooper, 1998). Although they are a fundamental aspect of social studies teaching and learning, are values and perspectives still the 'hard bits' of the subject, along with social decision making and action (Keown, 1998)? In this section we suggest that pedagogy has not kept pace with a shifting, emphasis over time, away from viewpoints and towards values and perspectives in New Zealand social studies curricula. To provide a backdrop to this, we begin by briefly outlining how viewpoints, values and perspectives have gained expression in successive curriculum statements.

The first social studies syllabus for primary schools (Department of Education, 1961) lightly incorporated the terms 'viewpoints' and 'values'. As a product of its time it had a whiff of 'them and us', given that it expected primary school children to "understand many points of view—both those that may be held by most of their fellow countrymen and the sometimes diverse views held by people of other countries" (p. 2). It was to be the introduction of the *Forms 1–4 Social Studies Syllabus Guidelines* (Department of Education, 1977) that positioned values as a central part of a process-focused curriculum, in which nine of 19 specific objectives were explicitly values education oriented. An overarching objective of this syllabus was that "social studies should help students to think clearly and critically about human behaviour and values so that they can make reasoned choices" (p. 9).

Values remained a strong component of the *New Zealand Curriculum Framework* (Ministry of Education, 1993), and subsequent draft social studies curriculum statements, although it was not until the 1997 social studies curriculum that the concept of perspectives was introduced (Ministry of Education, 1997). Teachers were expected to address five perspectives across all curricula: bi-cultural, multi-cultural, gender, current and future perspectives. These perspectives were ways to ensure social studies was not dominated by a male-WASPish[1] representation of society. While their curricular presence might reflect the postmodern turn in the wider social sciences, their somewhat limiting nature has been avoided in New Zealand's current social studies curriculum learning area statement. More recent curriculum support documents have encouraged the finer-grained analysis and naming of theoretical perspectives. For example, perspectives on globalisation could include ecological, neo-liberal, feminist, post-colonial and pro-globalist world views (Ministry of Education, 2009, 2013).

Since Keown's (1998) concerns in the mid-1990s, there has been evidence to suggest that values analysis continues to remain the hard bits of social studies. For example, an Education Review Office (2006) report notes that values exploration is often conflated with identifying points of view. An evaluation of the implementation of the *NZC* (Ministry of Education, 2007) highlights that only

> a small proportion of respondents report integrating values into learning experiences across the curriculum (22%), learning about the nature of values (17%), and developing skills for exploring values (15%). (Sinnema, 2011, p. 37)

Further, a Teaching and Learning Research Initiative (Notman et al., 2012) study indicates that teachers' perceptions of their students' ability to "critically analyse values and actions based on them" and "discuss disagreements that arise from differences in values and negotiate solutions" are low. We wonder whether implementation of the values statement at the front end of the curriculum (Ministry of Education, 2007, p. 10), and in particular the list of values to be encouraged, has meant that some schools are emphasising inculcation approaches. We also wonder whether this emphasis has to some extent disembodied the critical values analysis dimensions of curriculum learning areas. The subject richness of social studies, for example, is not simply the expression of personal values, or even the identification of other groups' values, but how values

---

1 The acronym for white, Anglo-Saxon, Protestant is used to signal dominant culture.

may be interpreted differently and change over time, and the implications that emerge when values systems collide (Gilbert, 2011).

In the case of perspectives, we contend that the central reason this appears to be one of the hard bits of social studies is a lack of appreciation of the force of the meaning of the concept as it is understood and applied in social studies. Words and concepts in any language often have subtle meanings that vary according to context. Those who develop school curricula need to use words that are congruent with the literature and the language of the disciplines that inform the content and processes of school subject. Herein lies a particular challenge for New Zealand social studies. While a subject in its own right, it draws upon a range of disciplinary traditions including economics, geography, history and sociology. Some of these disciplines use the concept 'perspectives' in ways that are highly specialised and have particular subject meanings. Social studies teachers may or may not have strong backgrounds in social science–humanities learning, and most secondary school teachers are likely to be a specialist in only one of the contributing disciplines.

This is a reminder that whatever the intended signposts/messages of social studies curricula, they are mediated by teachers who themselves have different opinions, values and world views about the nature and purpose of social studies (Aitken, 2005). The need for a shared understanding of viewpoints, values and perspectives—as they apply particularly to social studies—is a key message of this chapter.

Approaches to deepening thinking through viewpoints, values and perspectives

What people hold as important, and why, can be understood at greater levels of depth and criticality. Our task in this final section is to demonstrate that deepening thinking through viewpoints, values and perspectives need not be the preserve of secondary school. To do this, we offer some initial suggestions for lower levels of the curriculum, together with examples of viewpoints, values and perspectives that can be used as social studies-specific tools to deepen student thinking. Using secondary contexts, we then turn to exemplify how an understanding of perspectives can be derived from activities that are more usually associated with 'viewpoints', and how perspectives thinking can be linked to social action—another 'hard bit' of social studies.

We contend that even students working at lower levels of the curriculum are capable of developing critical thinking skills through their consideration of viewpoints, values and perspectives. For teachers working with pre-literate learners, the exploration of different viewpoints can be facilitated by 'thumbs up, sideways, or down' and 'smiley, straight, or sad face' approaches, so that productive language acquisition is not necessarily a barrier to the development of viewpoint learning. More sophisticated viewpoints work could involve interviewing others to create 'vox pops' on an issue, developing a mock social media account to express an opinion, or sorting and grouping viewpoints expressed in the media. When students can explain *why* people hold such viewpoints, they are beginning to move into an understanding of values.

At lower levels of the curriculum, students' skills in critically analysing values are often developed through class discussion. A values continuum, for example, can provide a stimulus for discussion in which students explore why there is values conflict in an issue. Social studies perspectives are undoubtedly complex concepts that involve greater cognitive demand. But here, again, students working at lower levels of the curriculum can begin to appreciate perspectives through the eyes of particular groups (e.g. 'Why is tūrangawaewae important from a te ao Māori perspective?' or 'How might girls think differently from boys about this?'). Understanding perspectives as world views is not beyond primary students, and Wood and Milligan (2010) have provided evidence that a careful approach to introducing perspectives can produce high levels of critical thinking, at least by Level 5 of the curriculum (see also Michael's vignette in Chapter 3).

What might perspectives thinking look like at higher curriculum levels? In the following two examples we first consider how a commonly used teaching strategy—cartoon interpretation—can be used to generate deeper levels of critical thought. We then explore a perhaps lesser-known narrative approach to show how perspectives thinking can be linked to considering decisions and responses, and social action. What is notable about both strategies is that they demonstrate how critical thinking about viewpoints, values and perspectives can be developed *in tandem*, rather than each being treated as tied to particular curriculum levels.

Example 1: Cartoon interpretation

The Western cultural motif of a stork notwithstanding, how might the cartoon in Figure 4.3 be approached by a teacher wishing to explore viewpoints, values and perspectives about resource management? In our view, this is an example of a cartoon that contains quite a clear viewpoint about resources being overburdened by population. Yet, deeper attention to values and perspectives gets students beyond the surface message of the cartoon to understand ecological, cultural and economic values. Deeper still, as the questions added to the cartoon suggest, differing 'sustainability' paradigms can be revealed.

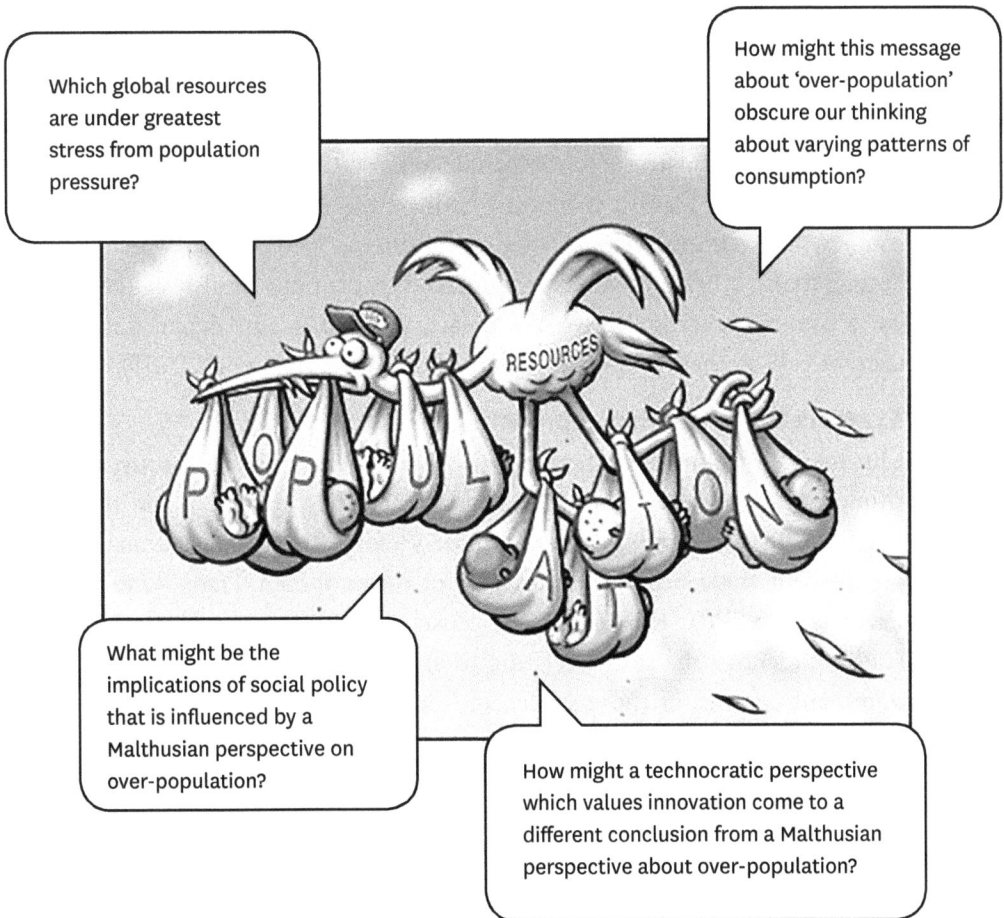

Figure 4.3: Exploring viewpoints, values and perspectives

Cartoon source: http://www.claybennett.com/pages/overpopulation.html

The cartoon echoes Thomas Malthus's 1798 *Essay on the Principle of Population*, which argued that the growth of food production could not keep pace with the exponential growth of population, predicting famine in those places where the burden of overpopulation was too severe. Since post-war increases in consumption rates and the retreat of colonial resource control, interest in the Malthusian perspective has rekindled (Linner, 2013). The Club of Rome's 1972 *Limits to Growth*, the (recently rescinded) Chinese one-child policy and Indian forced sterilisation, are social policy echoes of a neo-Malthusian world view. Popular recent best sellers such as Jarod Diamond's *Collapse* and Danny Dorling's *Population 10 Billion* also hint at lingering Malthusian perspectives.

However, engaging with Figure 4.3 also requires acknowledging that Malthusian perspectives are often considered doom-mongering, especially by those who take a far more positive view of the role of technology in mitigating environmental collapse. For example, readers may be aware of Danish economist Esther Boserup's "necessity is the mother of invention" critique of the Malthusian perspective, which, among many other individuals, groups and institutions, is also shared by a contemporary collective of scholars, scientists, campaigners and citizens calling themselves Ecomodernists (Asafu-adjaye et al., 2015).

Example 2: A narrative approach

Our second example of how viewpoints, values and perspectives thinking can be developed in tandem is a narrative approach, and to illustrate this we draw on the controversy over current international government trade negotiations as part of the proposed Trans-Pacific Partnership (TPP). The narrative approach is based on the idea that students identify the stories relating to an issue before describing the dominant features of those stories and deciding which story is more compelling for them.

In steps 1 to 3 in Table 4.1, the stories about the TPP are analysed at the level of viewpoints and values. In steps 4 to 5 the discourses that shape stories about the TPP are analysed through the lens of theoretical (including ethical) perspectives. And in the remaining steps the values and perspectives lead to social action as students devise a plan to give their preferred story more power. Milligan (2014) notes that the productive potential of the narrative approach is that it (a) highlights the effects of *overlapping* and contradictory perspectives on learners' viewpoints, values and actions; (b) prompts attention to diverse voices; and (c) enables a consideration of how 'stories' could offer exploration of alternative futures for students' lives.

Table 4.1: Taking a narrative approach to the proposed Trans-Pacific Partnership

Step	Typical focus	Inquiry questions
1. Topic/issue definition	Clarify and define a value-laden topic or issue for investigation and study.	The Trans-Pacific Partnership (TPP): What is proposed? For whom? Why?
2. Identify a range of stories (discourses) about this issue. *(Steps 2 and 3 can be reversed)*	Recognise there is a range of stories that are told about how things are and the way they should be in our classroom, school, community and society. Identify and describe some of them.	What are the different viewpoints on the proposed agreement? What do pro-TPP groups say? What do anti-TPP groups say? What kinds of language are being used? What does this tell us about what each group values?
3. Identify and describe the key features of the dominant story	Identify which story is the dominant one in the situation being studied.	What stories do these different groups tell? Which do you think is the dominant story? The one that most New Zealanders believe?
4. Deconstruct the stories	Discuss and analyse these views or discourses; dialogue about the merits of the various stories and perspectives; examine which stories are more powerful and which are less powerful, and why.	What are some of the possible perspectives that drive the beliefs and arguments of both sides? (For example neo-liberalism, capitalism, social justice, post-colonialism, social class, Marxism, sustainability, Indigenous)
5. Select a preferred story	Decide which story appears to be the best. *(Ethical criteria such as 'fairest to all concerned' or 'in the common good' will need to be used here.)*	The class may want to divide into different groups for this activity. Which story, narrative or discourse appears preferable for you? On what evidence?
6. Devise a plan to empower the preferred story	Consider how to give the preferred story more power. Devise strategies to publicise and encourage people to adopt the new story. Think of ways to support the new story as it grows and develops.	How could you convince people that the TPP is either a good thing or a bad thing? What argument could you use? What means of persuasion could you use?
7. Implement the plan	This includes putting the plan into operation and reviewing and adjusting it as necessary.	Try implementing your plan with friends, family, in the class, in your community. Which parts of your plan worked and which did not work? Adjust your plan and try again.

Conclusion

Viewpoints and values have been a longstanding component of New Zealand social studies education, designed to allow students to explore the complexity of societal issues and attendant decision making. While a focus on values inculcation and awareness promotes socialisation, social studies students' abilities to engage critically with societal issues require school curriculum-making that attends to the contested, fluid collision zones of different values systems. In this way students can be exposed to diverse rationales about how society should be organised and transformed.

Over the last 20 years the more challenging concept of 'perspectives' has been added to the social studies envelope. Having offered examples of what this could look like across curriculum levels, we suggest that the higher levels of critical analysis and synthesis associated with perspective thinking is a goal worth striving for. This is because an understanding of perspectives reveals the deeper-set aspects of *societal* controversy, values conflict and differing visions for social change—the very stuff of social studies learning.

Reflective questions

- What are the opportunities and challenges for inviting different voices into social studies focused classrooms?

- How might schools report on conceptual progression using a viewpoints, values and perspectives framework?

- Is there a relationship between viewpoints, values, perspectives and social action in social studies?

References

Aitken, G. (2005). *Curriculum design in New Zealand social studies: Learning from the past.* Unpublished doctoral thesis, University of Auckland.

Asafu-adjaye, J., Blomqvist, L., Brand, S., Brook, B., Defries, R., Ellis, E., et al. (2015). *An ecomodernist manifesto.* Retrieved from http://www.ecomodernism.org.

Burgh, G., Field, T., & Freakley, M. (Eds.). (2006). *Ethics and the community of inquiry: Education for deliberative democracy.* Melbourne, VIC: Cengage/Thomson.

Chandler, G. (1979). Some valuing strategies. In N. Zepke & R. Somerville (Eds.), *Approaches to social studies* (pp. 97–103). Wellington: Methuen NZ and Waikato Social Studies Association.

Crompton, T. & Weinstein, N. (2015). *Common cause communication. A toolkit for charities.* London: Common Cause Foundation.

Department of Education. (1977). *Social studies syllabus guidelines. Forms 1–4.* Wellington: Author.

Department of Education. (1961). *Social studies in the primary school.* Wellington: Government Printer.

Education Review Office. (2006). *The quality of teaching and learning in Years 4 and 8: Social studies.* Wellington: Author.

Fonterra. (2014). *Our promise.* Retrieved from http://www.fonterra.com/our-promise.

Gilbert, R. (2011). Working with values and controversial issues. In R. Gilbert & B. Hoepper (Eds.), *Teaching society and environment* (4th ed., pp. 79–98). South Melbourne, VIC: Cengage.

Holmes, T., Blackmore, E., Hawkins, R., & Wakeford, T. (2011). *The common cause handbook.* Retrieved from http://www.valuesandframes.org.

Keown, P. (1998). Values and social action: Doing the hard bits. In P. Benson & R. Openshaw (Eds.), *New horizons for New Zealand social studies.* Palmerston North: ERDC Press.

Keown, P., Parker, L., & Tiakiwai, S. (2005). *Values in the New Zealand curriculum: A literature review on values in the curriculum.* Report for the Ministry of Education, New Zealand by the Wilf Malcolm Institute of Educational Research, School of Education, University of Waikato.

Linner, B.-O. (2013). Commentary: Thomas R. Malthus, an essay on the principle of population (1798). In L. Robin, S. Sorlin, & P. Warde (Eds.), *The future of nature.* New Haven, CT, and London, UK: Yale University Press.

Milligan, A. (2014). *Transcending the ethically silent space of New Zealand's social studies curriculum.* Unpublished doctoral thesis, Victoria University of Wellington.

Ministry of Education. (1993). *The New Zealand curriculum framework.* Wellington: Learning Media.

Ministry of Education. (1997). *Social studies in the New Zealand curriculum.* Wellington: Learning Media.

Ministry of Education. (2007). *The New Zealand curriculum*. Wellington: Learning Media.

Ministry of Education. (2008). *Building conceptual understandings in the social sciences: Approaches to social inquiry*. Wellington: Learning Media.

Ministry of Education. (2009). *Building conceptual understandings in the social sciences: Being part of global communities*. Wellington: Learning Media.

Ministry of Education. (2013). *Points of view, values, and perspectives in senior social studies*. Retrieved from http://seniorsecondary.tki.org.nz/Social-sciences/Senior-social-studies/pedagogy/social-inquiry/Points-of-view.

Notman, R., Latham, D., Angus, H., Connor, P., McGregor, K., & Scott, J. (2012). *Integrating values in the New Zealand curriculum: Caught or taught?* Wellington: Teaching and Learning Research Initiative. Retrieved from http://www.tlri.org.nz/sites/default/files/projects/9292-summaryreport_0.pdf

Powney, J., Cullen, M., Schlapp, U., Glissov, P., Johnstone, M., & Munn, P. (1995). *Understanding values education in the primary school*. Edinburgh, UK: Scottish Council for Research in Education.

Rokeach, M. (1973). *The nature of human values*. New York, NY: The Free Press.

Scriven, M. (1966). *Primary philosophy*. New York, NY: McGraw-Hill.

Sharpe, M. (2015, 5 August). Judge blasts Fonterra for putting productivity ahead of the environment. *Stuff.* Retrieved from http://www.stuff.co.nz/environment/70844577/Judge-balsts-Fonterra-for-putting-productivity-ahead-of-the-environment.

Schwartz, S. H. (2006). Basic human values: Theory, measurement and applications. *Revue français de sociologie, 47*, 259–288.

Sinnema, C. (2011). *Monitoring and evaluating curriculum implementation: Final evaluation report to the Ministry of Education on the implementation of the New Zealand curriculum 2008–2009*. Auckland: University of Auckland.

Slater, F. (1993). *Learning through geography*. London, UK: Heinemann Educational Books.

Stevenson, J., Ling, L., Burman, E., & Cooper, M. (Eds.). (1998). *Values in education*. London, UK: Routledge.

Stevenson, R. B. (1987). Schooling and environmental education: Contradictions in purpose and practice. In I. Robottom (Ed.), *Environmental education: Practice and possibility.* (pp. 69–82). Melbourne, VA: Deakin University Press.

Strike, K. A. (1999). Can schools be communities?: The tension between shared values and inclusion. *Educational Administration Quarterly, 35*(1), 46–70.

Taylor, R., & Atkins, R. (2005). Putting the 'values' back into the values exploration process. In P. Benson & R. Openshaw (Eds.), *Towards effective social studies*. Palmerston North: Kanuka Grove Press.

Wood, B. E., & Milligan, A. (2010). Possibilities for summative assessment in social studies. *set: Research Information for Teachers, 2*, 17–24.

Chapter 5 Teaching social studies for social justice: Social action is more than just 'doing stuff'

Carol Mutch, Maria Perreau, Bronwyn Houliston and Jennifer Tatebe

Key points

- One of the aims of teaching social studies is to build students' awareness of social justice issues.
- Social inquiry is a common approach to teaching about social justice, but it often stops before authentic social action is undertaken.
- The proliferation of models of inquiry can be confusing.
- A simplified social inquiry for social action process can help teachers to have a stronger social justice focus

Introduction

> Yes I enjoyed taking the social action because we got to do something different and we also took the chance to raise awareness about obesity which is a major problem in our community. I loved it! (Year 10 student)

Students in today's classrooms face a world in which they will be confronted by choices and issues we might never have considered possible. *The New Zealand Curriculum* outlines our responsibility for preparing the next generation for this ever-changing, uncertain and volatile future. The Social Sciences learning area expects that we will help the students in our care to

> develop knowledge and skills to enable them to: better understand, participate in and contribute to the local, national and global communities in which they live and work; engage critically with societal issues; and, evaluate the sustainability of alternative social, economic, political and environmental practices. (Ministry of Education, 2007, p. 30)

Previous chapters have raised questions such as, 'How do we get students to critically engage in social issues?', 'How do we help them evaluate alternatives?' and 'How do we raise awareness of social injustice?'. As social studies educators we take these concepts seriously, but in the busyness of classroom life, as we aim to balance content and assessment expectations, we sometimes pay lip service to what teaching for social justice *really* means. In this chapter we suggest that social action is a way in which we can encourage students to critically engage in social issues and evaluate alternatives.

What our research has shown is that there are very few resources available to support teachers to help students to engage fully in relating issues of social justice to their own lives. Of those that do, many don't lead students to genuine social action. Take, for example, the New Zealand Qualifications Authority (NZQA)-approved NCEA Level 1 exemplar *Internal Assessment Resource Social Studies 1.4 v2 for Achievement Standard 91042* (Ministry of Education, 2012). In this achievement standard the social action is reflecting on personal involvement in an activity. Achieving the standard with excellence requires making suggestions for possible adaptations. In the exemplar, students develop awareness by engaging in a fundraising activity in which they cut out red cardboard hands. The exemplar for excellence states, "An alternative action would have been to get the students to make their own red hand print in paint to place on the sheet … but the possibility of students getting paint on their uniform or around the school made us reject this alternative as not being effective." Is this exemplar really promoting *critical engagement* and *social action*?

The authors of this chapter are a group of researchers and practitioners who want to share their ideas about making social action more than just 'doing stuff'. We want to inspire teachers at all levels to take that extra step towards critical and authentic social action. First, we discuss some key terms linked to social action. Next, we offer a way of incorporating social action into a typical planning cycle. To show what teaching for social justice might look like in practice, one of the authors then describes a social studies unit in which she incorporated social action into her planning, teaching and reflection. We conclude our chapter by reiterating the key ideas we have covered. Throughout the chapter we reference useful resources and suggest these as a starting point for teachers.

> I enjoyed the social action because it is something I'm passionate about and I'd keep this going as a group in our school. (Year 10 student)

Situating social action in a critical framework

The concepts of fairness, equity, social action and transformative change reflect theoretical conceptions of social justice within the critical tradition. *Critical theory* offers a lens through which to examine the ways in which social institutions and cultural dynamics create and maintain inequities in society (Kincheloe & McLaren, 2002). Critical theory underpins the thinking of the chapter authors in that it connects our work in teaching and research to broader societal and global contexts. At the same time, it challenges us to reflect on our identities, roles, positions and responsibilities in society (Anyon, 2009; Theophanous, 1994). We view education for social justice as an ongoing process that helps students to understand and respond to existing inequities in society. For us, teaching social studies through social inquiry and social action honours diversity, challenges inequity, and promotes the actions, practices and processes of a fair and inclusive society.

'Social justice' is an intensely contested and widely debated term. Varying understandings and uses of the term reflect equally diverse goals that traverse a wide spectrum of political and philosophical perspectives (Craig, Burchardt, & Gordon, 2008). Both NZQA and the

Ministry of Education provide definitions and guidance for teaching about social justice. NZQA describes social justice as "an outcome of social action taken to develop fair treatment and equity for all" (NZQA, 2010, p. 1). Social justice in this context is underpinned by two concepts: a human rights or 'equity for all' focus, and a personal involvement or social action focus. Social justice is also identified as a key concept within the Social Sciences learning area. The Level 6 achievement objective, for example, requires students to "understand how individuals, groups, and institutions work to promote social justice and human rights" (Ministry of Education, 2007, p. 30).

Approaches to citizenship education

Citizenship education encompasses ideas of participation and action for the good of society. Barr, Graham, Hunter, Keown and McGee (1997) suggested that citizenship education enables "young people [to] develop the ability to make informed and reasoned decisions for the public good as members of a culturally diverse democracy in a changing world" (p. 5). Westheimer and Kahne (2004) offer another useful perspective. Their study of citizenship education programmes found three types of approaches: those that promoted *socially responsible citizens*, those that promoted *participatory citizens*, and those that promoted *justice-oriented* citizens. The approaches in New Zealand align most closely with teaching for participatory and justice-oriented citizens (Wood, Taylor, & Atkins, 2013). Westheimer and Kahne (2004) describe participatory citizens as individuals who "actively participate in the civic affairs and the social life of the community" (p. 241), while justice-oriented citizens examine and critique the underlying "social, economic, and political forces" of social issues and injustices (p. 242). Banks (2008) extends the goals of citizenship education to include societal transformation. Through transformative citizenship education, which encompasses notions of democracy and civic participation, students are encouraged to

> develop the decision-making and social action skills that are needed
> to identify problems in society, acquire knowledge related to their
> homes and community cultures and languages, identify and clarify
> their values, and take thoughtful individual or collective civic action.
> (p. 135)

Citizenship is often taught through *inquiry learning*. Inquiry learning appears in many forms, from the approach in *The New Zealand Curriculum* (Ministry of Education, 2007), which views all stages of teaching and learning as an inquiry, to a range of integrated activities across the curriculum. In its simplest form, inquiry learning has students follow a line of investigation—sometimes of their own choice, at other times with guidance from a teacher as part of a class topic. They collate and process information and share their conclusions. In social studies, inquiry learning came to the fore in the mid-20th century as a challenge to viewing teaching as an act of transmission of knowledge, and instead seeing learning as a process of engagement in ideas (Mutch, 2008; Wood, 2013). Since then it has been through many iterations. Today it is a common approach in many curriculum areas, especially given the ease of access to material through information and communications technology.

Boyd and Hipkins (2012) note three types of inquiry seen in New Zealand schools: generic, disciplinary and hybrid. In social studies, Wood (2013) suggests a hybrid approach is used most, appearing as a *social inquiry*, which includes going beyond information processing to include an analysis of social issues. A challenge for social studies educators is how to create an environment that fosters critically informed citizens and invites social action. Social inquiry offers a way forward. Social inquiry is defined by the Ministry of Education (2008, p. 2) as "an integrated process for examining social issues, ideas and themes". Wood (2013) suggests that social inquiry is more than that: it "has a dual commitment to gaining deeper knowledge about society as well as knowledge, dispositions, and skills to participate in society" (p. 22).

Wood explains this further by elaborating on two strands: *informational* goals (understanding how society works and how inequity arises) and *transformational* goals (undertaking action in pursuit of a more equitable society). When teachers plan a social inquiry, Aitken and Sinnema (2008) suggest they consider: connecting the experience to students' lives and selecting resources the students can relate to; aligning the experiences to important outcomes; building and sustaining a learning community through dialogue and collaboration; and designing experiences that motivate and interest students.

Active citizenship is historically linked to the concept of *social action* (Wood et al., 2013), and social action is acknowledged as being a difficult and challenging aspect of the curriculum to teach (Keown, 1998; Wood et al., 2013). To demonstrate active citizenship, students are encouraged to "participate and take action as critical, informed, and responsible citizens" (Ministry of Education, 2007, p. 17). In *Approaches to Social Inquiry* (Ministry of Education, 2008), social action appears as "Considering responses and decisions" and the "So what?" and "Now what?" prompts in the latter stages of the social inquiry. The resource suggests teachers and students ask, "Now what might be done about it?" Possibilities might include letter writing, petition signing, tree planting, rubbish collecting or informing others (Ministry of Education, 2008). We want to stress that the action needs to be tied to addressing a social issue, and that the activity should be the beginning of a more committed approach to social justice, not an end in itself. By engaging with the systemic roots of inequality, we aim to empower students to take action to mitigate these inequalities and create sustained and transformational social change (Adams et al., 2013).

Finally, in our discussion of approaches to citizenship education we note *service learning* as an emerging area of interest for New Zealand educators with an interest in social justice education. Originating in the US, the concept of service learning aims to connect academic learning with community-based projects (Eyler, 2002). Advocates of service learning promote its ability to connect education (students, educators and schools) with the wider world through community engagement, democratic goals, social justice and citizenship (Giles & Eyler, 1994). Following the Canterbury earthquakes, for example, university students who participated in the Student Volunteer Army could put that experience towards a credit-bearing service learning course (O'Steen & Perry, 2012). What is most important in approaching significant social issues through service learning is recognising that it is not just about helping in the community: it is also about developing an awareness of systemic social inequities and how they might be addressed on a wider scale.

Terms such as 'social justice' and 'social action' have different meanings in different contexts. To lessen confusion we have outlined definitions of relevant terms in ways that align with social studies ideas. In this section we have provided working definitions of social justice, citizenship education, inquiry learning, social inquiry, social action and service learning in recognition of their close association with different approaches to citizenship education. The definitions set the scene for our discussion of fostering *social inquiry for social action* through social studies teaching.

> I enjoyed the social justice action because it was something we did to help our community and knowing that we did something like that gives me a good feeling. (Year 10 student)

Social inquiry for social action: Another approach to citizenship education

Designing a social studies programme with social justice at its core requires an approach to teaching and learning that explicitly and purposefully sets out to achieve social action for social justice. Westheimer and Kahne's (2004) study of different citizenship education approaches, discussed earlier, found that justice-oriented programmes do not necessarily produce citizens who take action, and that those with a focus on participation do not necessarily produce justice-oriented citizens. We argue that students must be given the opportunities and experiences, the skills and knowledge, both to take action in communities *and* to critically analyse societal structures in pursuit of social justice. To be effective, these dimensions of authentic participation and justice orientation must be explicitly integrated from the earliest planning stages.

Chapter 3 introduced social inquiry and its distinction from generic inquiry approaches. There are various approaches and templates for using a social inquiry process, and in this chapter we have distilled our own simplified model of *social inquiry for social action* from other constructs, such as *The New Zealand Curriculum* (Ministry of Education, 2007), *Approaches to Social Inquiry* (Ministry of Education, 2008), and the social sciences *Best Evidence Synthesis* (Aitken & Sinnema, 2008), and from the literature (e.g. Westheimer & Kahne, 2004; Wood, 2013).

We have also incorporated our own experiences of teaching for social justice. We have prioritised what we consider to be the essential elements, which include an initial stage where teachers consider the students' needs and interests, the content to be covered according to curriculum and assessment expectations, the time and resources available, and ideas for incorporating authentic, engaging and motivating activities. We also discussed how to engage students at this stage. We call this stage the *setting-up inquiry*.

The next stage is one that is often not well considered. In our experience some teachers move too quickly to a student-led activity when students have only a superficial understanding of the topic. In this stage the teacher has explicit goals in mind, which they teach or reinforce. Key skills are revisited and students are introduced to the background, context, content and concepts that give the study meaning and purpose. We call this stage the *teacher-led inquiry*. We also feel there could be opportunities to model social action at this stage of the inquiry. This prepares students for their independent or collaborative inquiries and avoids social action being seen as an end-of-unit add-on.

As students begin to grasp a deeper understanding of the issue under investigation, they are invited to consider what aspects they might wish to examine in more depth—considering not just what they can find out but what they could do to promote awareness, contribute to alleviating the concern or engage in useful action. This we call the *student-led inquiry*. It builds on what has been done in the teacher-led inquiry but can also move in new directions.

The final element we considered essential was time for a *reflective activity*. This, we felt, was often rushed and tacked on at the end. Again, reflection, as with social action, can be undertaken at earlier stages. It also needs to go beyond a surface level that just asks students what they liked or what they'd do differently next time, to what they learned about social injustice and ways it can be remedied, how they could take what they learned from this experience to other aspects of their lives, and how it might make them think or act differently in the future. We emphasise that reflection is not just something that teachers ask students to do, but a thoughtful and purposeful activity they engage in themselves. As Figure 5.1 indicates, however, this is not the end but merely the beginning of the next inquiry cycle.

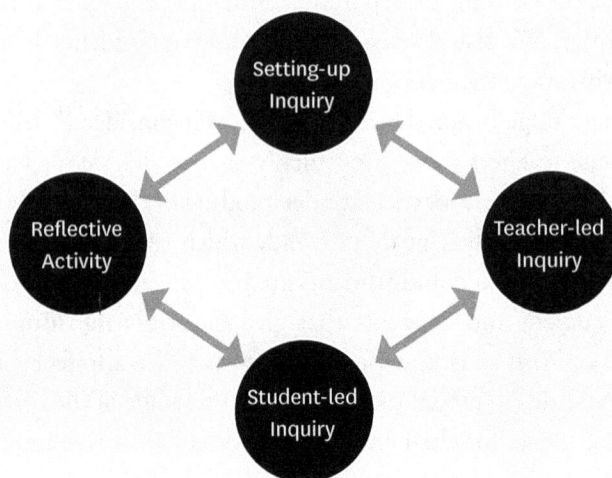

Figure 5.1: Social inquiry for social action

In the following section we reiterate the key aspects of each stage, providing advice to teachers from our teaching, reading and research.

The four stages in detail

The setting-up inquiry

In the planning stages it helps to view *both* teaching *and* learning as independent but inter-related inquiry processes. Aitken and Sinnema (2008) suggest that teachers have three complementary, overlapping inquiries happening: "a focusing inquiry, a teaching inquiry, and a learning inquiry" (p. 52). Their first two inquiries are important at the setting-up stage. The focusing inquiry has teachers consider what strategies might work best and what new approaches they might want to try. The teaching inquiry has teachers consider what is most important and therefore worth spending most time on—we think this is a significant consideration before too much planning gets underway.

To ensure social justice outcomes are embedded in the teaching and learning it is worth remembering Wood's (2013) informational goals and transformational goals. Questions addressing the *informational goals* might include:

- What theme, issue, resource or current event will be the catalyst for the learning inquiry?

- What sources will support an understanding of the context, content and concepts of the inquiry?
- What activities will assist students to access, evaluate, process and share information?
- What skills might be necessary to be taught or reinforced so that students can work on their inquiries independently or collaboratively?

Transformational goals might answer these questions:

- What aspects of society will be investigated and critiqued?
- Whose perspectives will be presented?
- What social action has already addressed, or is addressing, the issue?
- What contribution can students make to addressing this issue?

After matching ideas with curriculum and assessment expectations, teachers can establish the achievement outcomes and learning intentions for their students and decide how they will assess their students' knowledge and understanding of these. There might also be opportunities for student involvement in contributing to aspects of the setting-up inquiry.

The teacher-led inquiry

Moving to the second phase of the *social inquiry for social action* process involves focusing on how students are scaffolded to take on their own inquiries. Here the teacher uses the most effective strategies and resources in order to help students reach the intended outcomes by embedding key concepts and competencies into teacher-led activities that will provide a strong foundation for the later student-led inquiries.

One of the authors of this chapter investigated what resources were available for teaching for and about social justice in senior social studies in New Zealand (Perreau, 2014). Taking into account the relevant literature in social studies, citizenship and social justice education, she developed criteria to examine a selection of resources. Her criteria were *availability*, *accessibility*, *acceptability* and *adaptability*. The acceptability criteria, which align most closely to teaching for social justice, are outlined in Table 5.1.

Table 5.1: Acceptability criteria for resources for teaching social justice

Criteria	Questions to ask of resource
Acceptability	· Is **diversity** visible?
	· Is **knowledge** framed as contextual, contestable and changeable?
	· Are **contexts** relevant and are **connections** made?
	· Are successful **social justice** movements included?
	· Is a **critique** of society and its structure apparent?
	· Is there a focus on the integral role of **social action** in improving a democratic society?

Source: adapted from Perreau, 2014, p. 26.

In selecting resources and strategies that are available, accessible, acceptable and adaptable, Perreau claims, teachers can more effectively design learning experiences for and about social justice, and embed social action at the heart of the social inquiry process.

How teachers use resources is also important. Aitken and Sinnema (2008) remind teachers to begin by knowing their students: How do they learn? What do they already know? A variety of activities are then selected to align with the intended outcomes. Opportunities are provided to revisit learning processes and refine conceptual understanding. Milligan and Wood (2010) also emphasise the importance of building conceptual understanding. During the teacher-led inquiry the teacher is constantly reviewing how to engage students through relevant resources and activities, which build towards more sophisticated conceptual understanding. Conceptual understanding should also be seen as fluid and evolving. Useful questions for teachers at this stage might be:

• What are the big ideas that students need to grasp?

• What resources will enable students to understand the background to this issue?

• What sources will provide reliable information and different perspectives on this issue?

• What activities will help students to process multiple sources, gain deeper levels of understanding and refine their conceptual frameworks?

• How much time needs to be spent at this stage before students embark on their independent or collaborative inquiries?

Throughout the teacher-led inquiry it is helpful if students are exposed to examples of social actions that move beyond participatory to transformative. Examples can be drawn from historical or current events, works of fiction, film, drama, the arts or multimedia. Judiciously used, motivating resources provide opportunities to introduce and enhance conceptual understanding of social justice and social action (Tyson, 2002) and provide models of what is possible.

Student-led inquiry

Student-led inquiries that are purposeful, leading to social actions that are authentic, are strong foundations for beginning to understand the nature of our world. As Aitken and Sinnema (2008, p. 185) state, "First-hand experience of social, cultural, economic, and political situations makes learning real." Although some aspects of our world are complex and confusing, authentic learning experiences that lead to social action are not just for older or more able students. Aitken and Sinnema provide an example of children at an early childhood centre who took action to stop trolleys being taken from the local supermarket and abandoned in their neighbourhood. This also illustrates that the actions do not have to have global reach and deal with large-scale issues, but can be small acts that make a real difference to the local community.

Student-led inquiries, whether by individuals, pairs or groups, give students an opportunity to apply their skills to a real-life setting. They need to clarify the issue, gather and evaluate information, set out and select possible alternatives and put their plans into action. The teacher's role now focuses on teaching or reinforcing skills and knowledge that enable students to solve problems and move to the next step in their inquiry. The teacher also helps students to revisit and refine their ideas, linking them back to the teacher-led inquiry so that the developing conceptual understanding is deep and enduring (Ministry of Education, 2008).

Social inquiry questions can lead to meeting the *informational* goals as well as the *transformational* goals of social studies learning (Wood, 2013). Such questions therefore have two aspects and might look like this:

- What free leisure activities exist in our community for young people *and* how can we ensure access to them in the future?

- What opportunities for children's voices exist in our community *and* how can we be more involved in decisions that affect our lives?
- Are bees declining in our local community? Why does this matter *and* how can we help to increase the numbers of wild bees in our area?

There are many models of student-led inquiry processes. Again we have aimed to present a simplified process that can be adapted to different needs and interests. At its heart, however, is the desire to understand more about a social issue and undertake an action that might make a difference to this issue. Here are some guiding questions for teachers to adapt for their students:

- What is the problem or issue to be investigated?
- Why is this an issue and who is affected?
- What information is needed to understand the size and nature of the issue?
- What are some possible solutions?
- Which is the most workable solution for our context?
- In what ways could I (or my group) contribute to this solution?
- How do we put this into action?

For *social inquiry for social action* to work, the teacher also helps students move through and beyond participatory actions. Community participation is a useful stepping-off point and could be part of the teacher-led inquiry, but ultimately teaching for social justice requires understanding social issues as wider, often systemic and embedded, injustices. Here are some examples of how we have taken a selection of resources and suggest both participatory and transformative actions.

Table 5.2: Examples of participatory and transformational actions

Resource example	Participatory action	Transformative action
Stormwater education and action programmes (e.g. www.waicare.org.nz; www.enviroschools.org.nz)	Rubbish collection / litter pick-up	Interview community members about rubbish habits. Establish how litter gets into waterways and propose changes to the system so fewer people litter or illegally dump rubbish.
Community fruit harvest articles (multiple links on www.pickfuit.co.nz)	Volunteer to pick fruit, or make jams, sauces, etc, or donate fruit from your trees	Investigate the food supply chain from production to consumption. Critique the system, and propose an action plan to address the food supply issue at a structural level.
"Trade: Buying in or selling out?" (Levine, 2005). Or news articles on zero-hours contracts in New Zealand	Consumer actions: buy fair trade, boycott certain products or processes of production	Investigate the trade laws and regulations that perpetuate systemic injustices of workers. Propose legislation changes to protect workers.
Seedfolks (Fleischman & Pederson, 1997)	Plant trees, vegetables or flowers in the school grounds or in the local community	Meet with community members and the local council to investigate the possibility of space for a community garden for all to be involved and learn to grow food for themselves in small spaces.

In the *social inquiry for social action* process, the social action is the central focus of the inquiry from the outset. The setting-up inquiry, the teacher-led inquiry and the information processing part of the student-led inquiry all lead to undertaking an authentic and hopefully enduring action.

Reflective activity

Reflection is a key part of the social inquiry process for teachers and students alike. Reflection may be written—but it need not be. We suggest students choose how they reflect and teachers offer a variety of prompts for reflecting at various stages of the inquiry process. Sometimes reflections may be highly personal and independent; at other times they may be collective and expressive. What is significant is the process of reflecting: looking at what has been learnt, what it means in terms of understanding social justice, and how the experience influences their learning and their view of the social world. The ultimate aim is for students to see social issues not as fixed and insoluble, but as something in which they have a part to play in contributing to the solutions.

> I enjoyed the social action task because everybody contributed with the ideas, but next time extend our time so we can add more ideas. (Year 10 student)

Social action in practice

In this section one of the chapter authors outlines a social studies unit she taught with her Year 10 students at McAuley High School in Otahuhu, Auckland. As you will see, the stages of the social inquiry for social action process may overlap or be extended: the realities of the classroom in the context of a school are evident in this vignette.

At the end of term 4, my Year 10 social studies class and I embarked upon implementing social action within our community. From the beginning of this unit I decided that I wanted it to be student-led—that the students would identify the social justice issue they wanted to explore and that they would work together as a class to develop their social action. For me, this was an opportunity to develop not only student understanding of social justice but also their own sense of self efficacy.

Setting-up inquiry

Social justice is a concept that is often discussed at our school, but when it came to identifying the social action we could take within our community it quickly became apparent that I needed to clearly define social justice for my students. If social justice is an outcome of social action taken to develop fair treatment and equity for all people, then the students needed to clearly understand from the outset that any social action we took as a class needed to be more than fundraising or raising awareness: it needed to effectively address inequality within our community.

Teacher-led inquiry introduces social action as transformative

I showed my students an interview with the creator of "Humans of South Auckland", a Facebook page dedicated to changing negative perceptions of South Aucklanders. With this goal in mind, my Year 10 students were encouraged to look for examples of inequality in our local community. Students brought local newspapers to class and I also provided them with a range of articles that highlighted local issues. Groups of four to five students brainstormed the different issues that affect their community, using the articles as a basis but also drawing on their own understanding of the world around them, and shared them with the class on the whiteboard. The issues raised by my class included low educational achievement rates among Māori and Pasifika youth, stereotyping of South Aucklanders in the media, high rates of obesity within the community, and issues of youth suicide and domestic violence.

Teacher-led inquiry and emerging student-led inquiry

For many students the issue of obesity struck a personal chord. Obesity is a significant issue in South Auckland and often results in poorer health outcomes for members of our school community. My students also felt this was an issue for which they could develop a social action that was both sustainable and had the potential to effect real change. Once we decided as a class to target obesity, each group of four to five spent two to three lessons researching the issue further— identifying the different ways obesity affects our community. Our school nurse visited the class to discuss effective ways to target health issues within our school community. Students began investigating the physical consequences of obesity and subsequent strain on health services, while also considering the emotional and inter-generational issues that arise.

Students quickly identified that a key problem within our local community was the ability to access approachable information on healthy living that could be adapted to their lives. The students sought to solve this problem through social action. Possible social actions brainstormed in groups and on the whiteboard by the class were endless (and at times very ambitious!), and included running lunchtime exercise classes at school and creating a healthy recipe book for the school community.

I encouraged the students to develop success criteria for their action to help guide their choice, asking them, "What goal to do you want to achieve through your social action?" Students responded that they wanted to increase the activity levels of people in their community, encourage them to try healthy recipes and stop stereotyping based on weight. As a class they decided that their social action needed to be sustainable, have the potential for wide-ranging impact and the ability to be responsive to the community's health needs. Through a process of elimination the students decided that a blog, tailored to their school community, could be an effective way to meet these success criteria and help address health inequalities.

The students wanted the blog to provide accessible information to students and their families about how to live a healthy life (rather than focusing on just losing weight). As a class they identified a range of resources they could include on the blog, such as a recipe page, fitness videos, motivational music/playlists and printable documents. Very early on in the process a number of students also identified the need to translate key information on the blog into Māori, Samoan and Tongan so that it was accessible to as many members of our community as possible. The opportunity to work with multiple departments throughout the school, such as languages, P.E. and technology, during our social action also meant that the project had the potential to develop into interdisciplinary teaching and learning.

Students self-selected and split themselves into various groups according to the following interest areas:

- creating fitness videos using props that could be found around the school by the students

Student-led inquiry with ongoing teacher support

Social action identified and planned by students

- trialling and reviewing popular health and fitness apps, making recommendations for readers
- interviewing a staff member who had recently embarked on a healthy lifestyle change, creating a profile page on the changes she had made
- trialling healthy recipes with their families at home and sharing them on the website
- translating key information into Māori, Samoan and Tongan for the blog
- creating printable resources for readers to track their activity or plan their meals for the week.

Once in their groups they were left to allocate roles to individuals. This meant that once the social justice issue had been identified and the social action decided, the remaining lessons of the term were entirely self-directed.

Student reflections at the end of the unit were overwhelmingly positive. They enjoyed the opportunity to work as a class towards a common goal: looking for solutions to significant problems in their community and taking action to address them. The most import- **Reflective** ant piece of feedback the class gave me was that they wanted more **activity** time to take part meaningfully in the social action and see it through. Although some students felt rushed, many also saw the social action as something they could continue with in the future. Students felt that the process of learning about healthy living through the development of the blog had a positive impact on their lives, which they shared with their families. In their reflections the students indicated that they were hungry for opportunities to contribute to their community and develop a sense of empowerment. Bringing social justice into the classroom provides students with an opportunity to do just that.

> Yes I enjoyed it. It would have been cool to cook the recipe, but we probably didn't have any time. Also it would've been better to have more time to work on the social action and develop our website more. (Year 10 student)

Conclusion

Through the model of *social inquiry for social action* we have provided our ideas on what authentic learning for social justice might look like. We have shared our collective experiences from teaching, reading and research in the hope that we can inspire teachers to approach social inquiry with renewed enthusiasm. Our hope is that students will see transformative social action as more than 'just doing stuff'.

In this chapter we provided working definitions of key terms before outlining a four-stage social inquiry cycle. The cycle begins with a *setting-up inquiry*, moves to a *teacher-led inquiry*, which provides the necessary knowledge and skills for students to undertake a *student-led inquiry*, before completing the cycle with a *reflective activity*. We then described a social inquiry undertaken with a Year 10 class that illustrates some of the key points we are making about the teacher's role, the nature of the student-led inquiry and, finally, the importance of issues that relate to students' lives and offering them the chance to make a difference to their own community.

We acknowledge, along with other writers, that social justice-oriented action takes time (Kahne & Westheimer, 2006; Wood et al., 2013). In our busy schools and classrooms, where units of work are often between 5 and 8 weeks long, we cannot expect students to take actions that will correct systemic injustices, but we can inspire them to begin an initiative that, over time and with collective effort, could make a real difference. If we connect important social issues to students' lives and give them the confidence and competence to begin to address them, our citizens of tomorrow will be better equipped to make their world a better place for all.

Reflective questions

• How do you currently engage students in learning about issues of social justice?

• In what ways do you currently engage students in authentic social action?

• What changes could you make as a teacher, department and school as a result of the ideas in this chapter?

• What is the role of students in planning and implementing social inquiries for social action?

• What is the role of social studies in transformative social action?

References

Adams, M., Blumenfeld, W., Castaneda, C., Hackman, H. W., Peters, M. L., & Zuniga, X. (Eds.). (2013). *Readings for diversity and social justice* (3rd ed.). New York, NY: Routledge Taylor & Francis Group.

Aitken, G., & Sinnema, C. (2008). *Effective pedagogy in social sciences / Tikanga ā iwi: Best evidence synthesis iteration*. Wellington: Ministry of Education.

Anyon, J. (2009). Critical social theory, educational research, and intellectual agency. In J. Anyon (Ed.), *Theory and educational research: Toward critical social explanation* (pp. 1–23). New York, NY: Routledge.

Banks, J. A. (2008). Diversity, group identity, and citizenship education in a global age. *Educational Researcher, 37*(3), 129–139. doi: 10.3102/0013189X08317501.

Barr, H., Graham, J., Hunter, P., Keown, P., & McGee, J. (1997). *A position paper: Social studies in the New Zealand school curriculum.* Hamilton: School of Education, University of Waikato.

Boyd, S., & Hipkins, R. (2012). Student inquiry and curriculum integration: Shared origins and points of difference. *set: Research Information for Teachers, 3*, 15–23.

Craig, G., Burchardt, T., & Gordon, D. (Eds.) (2008). *Social justice and public policy: Seeking fairness in diverse societies.* Bristol, UK: Policy Press.

Eyler, J. (2002). Reflection: Linking service and learning—linking students and communities. *Journal of Social Issues, 58*(3), 517–534.

Fleischman, P., & Pedersen, J. (1997). *Seedfolks.* New York, NY: HarperCollins.

Giles, D., & Eyler, J. (1994). The theoretical roots of service-learning in John Dewey: Towards a theory of service-learning. *Michigan Journal of Community Service Learning, 1*(1), 77–85.

Kahne, J., & Westheimer, J. (2006). Teaching democracy: What schools need to do. In E. W. Ross (Ed.), *The social studies curriculum: Purposes, problems, and possibilities* (3rd ed., pp. 297–316). Albany, NY: State University of New York.

Keown, P. (1998). Values and social action: Doing the hard bits. In P. Benson & R. Openshaw (Eds.), *New horizons for New Zealand social studies* (pp. 137–159). Palmerston North: ERDC Press.

Kincheloe, J., & McLaren, P. (2002). Rethinking critical theory and qualitative research. In Y. Zou & E. Trueba (Eds.), *Ethnography and schools: Qualitative approaches to the study of education* (pp. 87–138). Lanham, MD: Rowman & Littlefield Publishers.

Levine, A. (Ed.) (2005). Trade: Buying in or selling out? *Just Change, 2.* Retrieved from http://www.globalfocus.org.nz/wp-content/uploads/2014/04/Just_Change_2.pdf.

Milligan, A., & Wood, B. (2010). Curriculum understandings as transition points: Making sense of a complex social world. *Journal of Curriculum Studies, 42*(4), 487–501. doi: 10.1080/00220270903494287.

Ministry of Education. (2007). *The New Zealand curriculum*. Wellington: Learning Media.

Ministry of Education. (2008). *Building conceptual understandings in the social sciences: Approaches to social inquiry*. Wellington: Learning Media.

Ministry of Education. (2012). *Internal assessment resource: Social studies 1.4A v.2*. Retrieved from http://ncea.tki.org.nz/Resources-for-Internally-Assessed-Achievement-Standards/Social-sciences/Social-studies/Level-1-Social-studies.

Mutch, C. A. (2008). "Creative and innovative citizenry": Exploring the past, present and future of citizenship education in New Zealand. In D. L. Grossman, W. O. Lee, & K. J. Kennedy (Eds.), *Citizenship curriculum in Asia and the Pacific* (pp. 197–214). Hong Kong: Springer Verlag.

NZQA (New Zealand Qualifications Authority). (2010). *Achievement standard AS91042*. Retrieved from: http://www.nzqa.govt.nz/nqfdocs/ncea-resource/ achievements/ 2011/as91042.pdf.

O'Steen, B., & Perry, L. (2012). Service-learning as a responsive and engaging curriculum: A higher education institution's response to natural disaster. *Curriculum Matters, 8*, 171–183.

Perreau, M. (2014). *Resources for and about social justice in senior social studies: Conceptions and disparities*. Unpublished master's dissertation, University of Auckland.

Theophanous, A. (1994). *Understanding social justice: An Australian perspective* (2nd ed.). Melbourne, VIC: Elikia Books.

Tyson, C. (2002). "Get up offa that thing": African American middle school students respond to literature to develop a framework for understanding social action. *Theory and Research in Social Education, 30*(1), 42–65.

Westheimer, J., & Kahne, J. (2004). What kind of citizen?: The politics of educating for democracy. *American Educational Research Journal, 41*(2), 267–269.

Wood, B. (2013). What is a social inquiry?: Crafting questions that lead to deeper knowledge about society and citizenship. *set: Research Information for Teachers, 3*, 20–28.

Wood, B., Taylor, R., & Atkins, R. (2013). Fostering active citizenship through the New Zealand social studies curriculum: Teachers' perceptions and practices of social action. *New Zealand Journal of Educational Studies, 48*(2), 84.

Chapter 6 Paying attention to emotions: Understanding the affective dimension in the social studies classroom

Rachel Tallon

Key points

- The emotional or affective dimension that students bring to the social studies classroom needs to be appreciated by teachers as an asset, not a deficit.
- Acknowledging students' emotions in social studies learning can lead to fruitful discussions and learning.
- Mapping the interplay of emotions through a theoretical lens can help teachers understand the role of emotions in an issues-based social studies classroom.

Introduction

Scenario

The news headline grabs your attention. A large New Zealand clothing manufacturer has been accused of poor labour practices: running sweatshops in South East Asia. The newspaper has run a special issue on the dilemmas of fashion, with articles urging people to check their clothing is sweatshop-free to put pressure on the New Zealand companies to lift their game. You decide this would be ideal to cover in social studies because it involves valuable concepts such as human rights, globalisation, consumer power, the media and law. You begin thinking about learning outcomes and what resources you might need. You're aware that one outcome is that your students become more ethical clothing shoppers. You can see a goal: by raising awareness about social injustice, knowledge will lead to action. Your students can make a difference and they can be empowered.

As a lesson like this proceeds, the learning *about* sweatshops may not necessarily evoke feelings of empathy *for* sweatshop workers. Some students may remain disconnected from the issues and the people affected by them. In looking to connect students' hearts with their heads, teaching can become reliant on evoking the affective dimension. This can cause teachers to question their pedagogy and the use of emotions to achieve certain ends.

This chapter addresses the pedagogical issue of engaging emotions for specific learning outcomes in social studies. Taking the scenario above, students may start to feel in ways the teacher desires: angry at such injustice, empathy with the workers, and a new-found desire to check their clothes are sweatshop-free. It is, however, just as possible that a different set of emotions come into play: lack of interest, boredom and cynicism, to name a few. As part of my own educational journey I have questioned what forces are at work in the classroom that can cause emotions to surface (Tallon, 2012). Many teachers have experienced the force of emotions as part of a school learning environment and have been left puzzled but impressed at this power. Reactions by teachers such as "They seemed really moved …" or, the opposite, "I can't get them to care", or "I wouldn't touch that topic because they'd get too heated" reveal acknowledgement of emotions, but they can be seen as mysterious, unmanageable and even feared. Sometimes luck comes into it when teachers cannot readily identify how the emotions are at work: "Today they were feeling sympathetic towards the issue, but on Monday they couldn't have cared less."

This chapter takes the premise that emotions are present in all classrooms—experienced by both the teacher and the students and affected by the formal context of the classroom. In social studies, in particular, emotions are often an integral part of the content and the contexts we teach. How can we teach about genocide or child labour in a dispassionate way? Often we demand, either consciously or not, an emotional response from our students, and it is this pedagogical intent that deserves special attention.

In this chapter, I aim to:

- highlight the significance of emotions in social studies learning in order to consider how they influence classroom discussions and responses to social issues and action

- discuss how theorists in this area help us to have a deeper understanding of the place of emotions in the classroom

- raise issues that arise from the misuse—intentional or not—of the direct evocation of emotions in the classroom

- bring these ideas together so that teachers can evaluate the power of emotions in their classrooms and consider how social studies should acknowledge the whole learner—their feelings, knowledge and subjectivities—and how these affect learning.

Theorist Megan Boler (1999) has explored both the absence and presence of emotions in the classroom, noting that emotions are often sought as part of learning yet never fully acknowledged or articulated in that learning process. An emotional reaction is often a hidden element of informal assessment and a source of evaluation by teachers of their own ability to engage their students. In social studies, the exploration of social issues, often with a view towards social action, taps into deeper, more ideological and emotive aspects of knowing. This may involve an evaluation of a value position or world view, something that may not have been carried out before by learners, and may involve an emotional engagement with a topic. Understanding their learners' personal emotional status as well as their embodied relationship to the classroom context can help teachers see how learning can be affected in many ways by emotions.

Part 1: The significance of the affective dimension in students and in social studies

Since the 1970s a focus on the affective domain, including values and moral education in the social studies curricula, has waxed and waned in New Zealand. In the 1977 curriculum students were asked to "think, feel and act" on their learning about social issues. Social studies curricula since then have consistently endorsed the exploration of values, which is likely to include the development of affective responses such as empathy. Yet this expectation is not explicitly referred to in curriculum documents despite that fact that "affective" outcomes are recognised as one of the five outcomes sets in social science learning (Aitken & Sinnema, 2008), and that often the most transformative and memorable moments in teaching come when the emotional, rather than the cognitive, aspects take centre stage (Sheppard, Katz, & Grosland, 2015).

While the importance of engaging with the emotional terrain in social studies is widely recognised (Sheppard et al., 2015), this is still often sidelined in social studies education due in part to several issues. First, teachers often ignore the taboo subjects (often related to sex, religion and cultural conflict) and stick to those that are more objective (Evans, Avery, & Pederson, 1999; Keown, 1998; Wood, 2007). Second, the discipline itself has been criticised for falling under a Cartesian spell (Baum, 1996), in that less rational and more emotional ways of knowing are not given the same space. Emotion can be marginalised by a focus on cognitive learning. With reference to social studies, Milligan (2014, p. 68) reflects that, as a rule, New Zealand curriculum documents

> hint at learners' consideration of ethical decision-making and action [but] emotional, embodied dimensions of ethical life are occluded by a prevailing ethos of reason, distance and objectivity.

This means that teachers might approach a topic such as the Holocaust from various angles, using literature and historical detail, for example, but they may avoid talking about psychological or interior emotions that students may be experiencing when learning about the topic. Baum (1996) would argue that this is because emotions are often viewed as private and not for scrutiny or discussion.

Third, in keeping with the safe option of distancing the emotional response, Evans et al. (cited in Sheppard et al., 2015, p. 149) found that teachers often default to choosing topics that are greater in distance from students' lives and thus reduce the chances of controversy. It is almost as if unpacking our responses to issues close at hand is too much of a Pandora's Box, which might cause delays in teaching a topic or produce unwanted outcomes. With these issues in mind, I turn now to examine more closely the role that emotions play in the social studies classroom.

Understanding emotions in the classroom

There has been a lack of theoretical understanding of emotions in the social studies classroom, but there has been growing acknowledgement of the increasing tendency in society towards "greater and greater engineering of affect" (Thrift, 2004, p. 64). This often refers to the use of empathy to move people to concern. Within social studies heightened calls for social action have been accompanied by the use of methods to engage the heart to inspire action. In social studies, emotions are likely to be most recognised as feelings associated with examining social issues, and in particular those concerning injustice and human stories. It is not enough just to 'learn the stuff', as in maths or English. Teaching about the injustices of human society may engender the creation of a certain identity and image. In social studies, certain values—especially those that are more politically progressive and tolerant—are either explicitly or implicitly promoted as an outcome of the learning. This can create expectations that learners are meant to feel and respond in a certain desired way to certain issues, topics or contexts they are studying.

Theorists such as Sara Ahmed (2004), Megan Boler (1999) and Michalinos Zembylas (2007) have researched how emotions operate in the classroom. Ahmed argues that emotions are both bound and created within social and cultural contexts, and within the context of the classroom there are certain rules and norms prescribing what can be felt and expressed. Zembylas believes that emotions are also deeply relational and not easy to predict or control. In agreement with Ahmed, he argues that emotions can also be performative, an outcome of how the embodied experience of something results in an emotional experience.

Sheppard et al. (2015, p. 153) point out that conceptualising emotions as "individual, dynamic and social, embodied and powerful, reveals the conflicting expectations and assumptions of emotions' role in teaching and learning." Within social studies, teachers need to be aware of the powerful ways emotions shape learning, identities and dispositions in the classroom. Bringing together how emotions such as empathy, pity and compassion intersect with social studies learning is a complex task. A triangle diagram (Figure 6.1) can help explain Ahmed and Zembylas's theorising about the inter-related emotive response to the content being taught. This conceptualisation shows how the learner brings to any issue their personal, relational and contextual response.

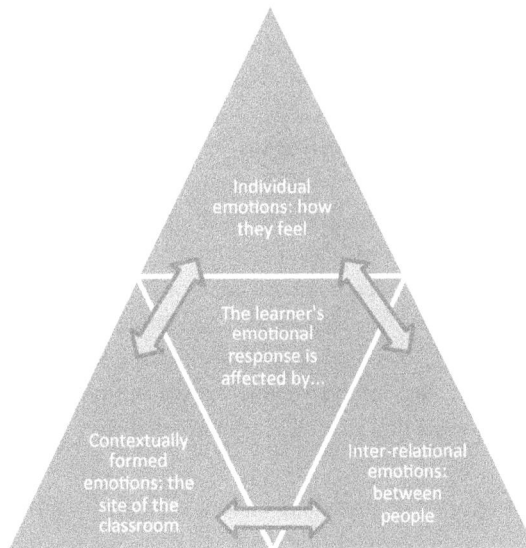

Figure 6.1: Mapping the relations of emotion in the classroom

Just as each learner brings their own emotions, they also relate emotionally to the teacher and their peers, and the context of the classroom also affects their emotions. The result is a new way of thinking: emotions are not confined *in* a learner, nor are they *in* a classroom. Instead, they are the product of the interactions—the green arrows in the diagram—which both constrain and create emotions (Wood & Taylor, 2016). The question is, how and where does pedagogy fit into this figure? In what way is the power of the teacher, topic or resource affecting the interplay of emotions present? The following part discusses issues that arise from either ignoring or manipulating one or all parts of the contributing triangles. The outcomes of this poor pedagogy or under-acknowledgement are then discussed.

Part 2: Key issues arising from mismanaged or misunderstood emotions in the classroom

Having mapped how emotions might be present in the context of the classroom, this part outlines three inter-related issues that often limit the learning potential in social studies due to emotions being marginalised or misused. To begin this part a case study by teacher-educator Michalinos Zembylas is given, followed by a discussion of three related issues.

Case study

Michalinos Zembylas (2012) reflects on an incident that occurred while teaching adult educators about multiculturalism and the benefits of diversity in Greek Cyprus. In the presentation he showed some examples of racist behaviour by Cypriots towards immigrants. After class he was approached by some of his students, who argued that he was "too immigrant friendly" and was "Greek Cypriot bashing" (p. 115). Upon reflection he recognised that he had sympathised entirely with the immigrants, while "completely ignoring the feelings of those who saw their country changing so rapidly" (ibid). He reflected that he needed to more explicitly address the emotional aspects of these responses as a form of "troubled knowledge" rather than dismiss them as "wrong" or racist (Zembylas, 2012). Troubled knowledge is knowledge that is troubling or discomforting for different reasons for different groups in a community. Their values and viewpoints are at odds with those in power, such as the teacher.

The significance of Zembylas's case study and resulting reflection for this paper is to consider how educators can engage with the emotional terrain and "troubled knowledge" in the classroom and use it strategically rather than dismiss it as tangential or risky. Zembylas notes two aspects. First, there can be a separation of the current issue (such as national identity) from the negative connotations (such as racism). The two are not necessarily conjoined, although media often conflates them, making it difficult to discuss an issue without making it a personal attack. Second, people who hold such views that might appear non-progressive or radical in some way need to be humanised, not negatively pigeon-holed. Zembylas encourages teachers to explore and work with the emotions in the classroom, but there are a number of issues which mean that teachers often find this difficult to achieve. I explore three of these issues, outlining why they present difficulties and some possible ways to address them.

Issue 1: Controversial or 'hot' issues

In the beginning of this chapter I mentioned one of Sheppard et al.'s (2015) findings that there are taboo subjects that teachers avoid as a way of not tackling any emotional engagement, in case there are unwanted perspectives and emotional energy that cannot be contained. In the social studies classroom many teachers are apprehensive about various topics that might be contentious or 'laden with values' that are hard to pin down. Learners may align themselves with certain values they have not fully worked through for themselves. In addition, their values or those of the teacher may not match those of the school or community.

Keown (1998) addresses this problem of putting values and action into the too-hard basket by arguing that values and action are at the core of social studies. Social studies has been negatively affected by the "scientific management" of the topic, which seeks to rationalise content and avoid controversial topics. Wood (2007) argues that this is because of "the slippery stuff": values, opinions and feelings about issues that are difficult to quantify, difficult to assess and could cause unbidden emotions to surface. Yet they are the building blocks for critical and creative thinkers, and along with Keown, Wood makes the case that social studies should not focus on the facts and the knowledge, but have as a *core learning outcome* the skills of learning how to deal with different values and to negotiate our own positions with those of others. In short, we need to think critically about ourselves and others without the need to withdraw behind defensive barriers.

Learning the pedagogical skills to support this aim is difficult, because it is also very contextually driven. A teacher needs to be more of an artist than a technician. Their management strategies may call upon acting skills more than just how to run a discussion. Lindquist (2004) observes that when teachers depart from the script, from the *control* of emotions, they make room for discussions that can be freer than normal. Above all, they need to adapt their pedagogy so that they can feel skilled in showing how tackling some of the more difficult issues in society is important and not for the too-hard basket. Michael Harcourt (Chapter 3) gives an example of changing tack and approaching a topic from a new angle to develop interest by engaging directly with the emotions students conveyed about studying the Treaty of Waitangi.

Issue 2: The emphasis on rational thinking

One of the key reasons for a historical lack of attention to the emotive work that is carried out in the classroom has been the emphasis on rationality. This is related to the above issue, but this emphasis paints emotion as a deficit. The classroom is situated in a (mostly) secular environment, whereby emotions and feelings have often been divorced from and silenced in the knowledge setting.[1] Reason, especially through a focus on critical thinking, can be accused of usurping belief so that faith or emotions are cast in a negative light—a shadow of the 'truth' of science or progressive ideals. Lindquist (2004, p. 190) argues that instead of maintaining this duality—whereby you can only express your emotions and faith outside of the classroom, a kind of divorcing of the heart from the head—teachers need a much better understanding of how affective dimensions shape their students' learning. Lindquist calls for a "puzzling out" of the emotions that learners bring to the classroom involving an inclusion of how they feel emotionally, physically and spiritually as an integral aspect of viewing them as "whole" people, not just empty minds.

It can be difficult for students to transcend their ordinary lives and try to imagine being in someone else's shoes and find some form of empathetic engagement with that person. In other words, learning does not take place solely in the head: the heart is in it too. Critical thinking or critical reflection is embedded in many social studies classrooms and is often used as a tool to understand social injustices. This method may cause a distancing from lived experience: we can 'know' an issue and critique it, without truly appreciating how or why we relate or do not relate to the issue ourselves.

Issue 3: Fears of emotional manipulation and predetermined learning outcomes

One further reason that teachers are reluctant to engage in emotional and affective aspects of social studies learning is the fear of being accused of emotional manipulation. In the New Zealand context, Keown (1998, p. 140) has raised this issue, noting that "The fear of being accused of indoctrination or social engineering is never far from the minds when teachers are contemplating the values and social action dimensions of social studies." My own doctoral research began with considering how captive audiences, such as students in a classroom who cannot easily choose to be elsewhere, can be emotionally led on a trajectory towards a specific emotive outcome that is meant to result in a desired outcome, such as feelings of empathy towards people facing

---

1   The exception is faith-based schools, which may welcome aspects of spirituality more readily than secular state schools.

difficult times. This is perhaps the extreme end of emotional manipulation and is often not fully acknowledged as occurring, although intuitively teachers can often sense when they are being campaigners rather than educators. Sharon Todd (2009) notes that as educators we can fall into teaching for a world that is *not yet*, a form of utopia which we hope to bring about through our individual or collective actions. As teachers of social studies seeking to transform our students into active citizens, we can be too focused on the 'should be' rather than the 'what is'. We want our students to feel and then act in positive ways that bring about a better world, but this carries a risk, as Todd notes:

> in educating *for* humanity, we run the risk of creating for children
> a world which does not respond to it *as it is*, and create instead a
> harmonious image of what we adults *want the world to be*.
> (Todd, 2009, p. 16, emphasis in original)

This harmonious image is often presented in the class, and learners can be given tools, such as a discrete form of social action, to help make a difference. However, the brushing over of the world 'as it is' is part of this denying of troubled knowledge, the emotions and concerns that learners bring to the classroom that may be contrary to what is being presented. With reference to the earlier example of Zembylas, he had a predetermined world that he was aspiring to in his course. He wanted his students to become tolerant and work towards a racially harmonious society. By reflecting on his students' troubled knowledge, he reassessed his goals. Instead of creating 'model Zembylases', he recognised that he needed to help form citizens who were not afraid of asking questions. He moved from being a campaigner to an educator.

Instead of overt (or covert) campaigning or awareness raising, educators can actively equip learners to participate in the debate. This might entail encouraging learners to ask questions of the teacher and themselves and to think widely and critically concerning an issue, but also to consider their emotional response. Sheppard et al. (2015, p. 161) discuss how a teacher in a religiously influenced school environment struggled to create a truly democratic discussion of certain controversial issues, due to the underlying ideology of the school foreclosing any alternative ideas. Instead of pushing ahead in one direction, the teacher acknowledged that communal emotions play a role in boundary forming to protect what is valued, a similar finding to that made by Zembylas. Instead of trying to remove or negate those limits, a better way forward may be to affirm those emotions so that learners can remain open to new ideas without having to expend energy protecting their own. Identifying communal ideologies that affect how we emotionally engage is a fertile area worth exploring.

These three issues are closely related and together illustrate common reasons why teachers sometimes avoid engaging with the affective aspect of social studies teaching and learning. In Part 3 I discuss how not acknowledging emotions carries risks that affect learning.

Part 3: The risks of not taking emotions seriously in social studies

In this final part I present three potential risks arising from either failing to engage with emotions or attempting to engage with emotions but doing so poorly. Both positions risk jeopardising the quality of learning in social studies, as well as reducing critical understandings of society.

Outcome 1: Superficial and transitory concern

If learners are given little choice but to follow a specific emotional trajectory, they may respond with superficial learning or responses and only transitory concern for any social issue. This surface response is problematic. Unless a student can relate to an issue they are likely to be less interested, less engaged (Aitken & Sinnema, 2008). Schön argues that teachers can come to see themselves as depositors of higher or more abstract knowledge, which lies almost outside of themselves, without being fully aware of how this is being received and enacted upon by their learners (as cited in Milligan, 2014, p. 131). When we explore everyday ethical dilemmas as well as more distant ones as part of social studies, there can be a tension between what the learner is thinking and constructing in their minds (even if they are just bored with the issue) and the new knowledge (including solutions) the teacher is imparting. When the teacher apparently occupies higher ethical ground, the learner may hide their messy knowledge, feelings, doubts and preferred actions and present an acceptable 'face' to the teacher. The learning that actually occurs involves mastering the art of deceit: hiding one's true feelings.

Outcome 2: Burnt emotions

As part of this surface reaction, a learner may encounter difficulty trying to achieve the emotions or actions that are expected. If empathy is not easily forthcoming, learners may consider themselves to be at fault. They may see themselves as heartless. Why can they not care for these people who are experiencing such injustice? Many learners do not wish to be seen as cold and unfeeling, but when they cannot acquire the preformed subjectivity of a caring person they may feel doubly bad. This is compounded if any action proffered is unrealistic.

In my own research (Tallon, 2013) the very real poverty of the Year 10 students that I interviewed precluded their appreciation of purchasing (expensive) ethical products, which was suggested as social action to reduce global poverty. They knew their teacher wanted them to buy certain products, but their daily lived reality meant this was impossible. This disconnect meant that although they sympathised with the intent, they grew frustrated at their impotence and felt they disappointed their teacher's ideals. The unachievable *emotional* learning outcome or lack of empathy meant that their actual learning outcome was disempowerment and, to a degree, disillusionment with themselves and the idea of social action. Thus, initial positive feelings about social injustice turned negative, because although they wanted to help, they had been placed in a situation whereby they realistically could not. This was unacknowledged and left them feeling morally deficient, which in turn led to further frustration. This negative cycle of feelings has been researched elsewhere, but mostly with adult participants (Seu, 2010, Hibbert, Smith, Davies & Ireland, 2007).

Outcome 3: Boxing on and missing the point

If the teacher does not get the desired emotional response, the response that does occur should be supported and explored. For example, in my research (Tallon, 2013) I came across an interesting scenario whereby a Year 10 social studies student in a focus group complained that her teacher "went on and on" about the civil unrest occurring at the time in the Middle East. The student was bored by these events and yet she knew she was meant to present an interested response, even if just by clicking on a web link in support of the uprisings.

To take up Zembylas's learning point, the teacher needed to explore students' responses to the learning as a vital part of social studies learning, rather than just boxing on. Questions might include: Why are we bored with what is happening over there? Why are their troubles taking up so much of our media time? Why do we flick to another channel for light entertainment rather than watch the news? Here the response to the issue is under the spotlight, and this throws open a new set of questions that allow the student to reflect on how distant events affect them, rather than the events themselves. This pedagogical shift acknowledges the state of the student first, and then reframes the learning outcomes of the lesson to include affective as well as cognitive dimensions.

Wood (2015) argues that being attuned to moments of emotional resistance or disengagement is important for generating new forms of learning. Blank stares and grunts of boredom are a valid response. Attentiveness to these responses requires an open and more flexible pedagogical approach by the teacher. Instead of disappointment, or a sense of loss, there is opportunity for learning to occur in a different direction. A truly democratic classroom allows for a range of responses and treats each with sensitivity—respecting the dignity of the learner.

Critics may argue that this does not help students learn about issues, but by not engaging with how a young person is disposed towards an issue, by just 'boxing on', little learning takes place and, at worst, surface or negative attitudes can develop, as described above. All responses are valid: they reflect where a learner is coming from and how they are interacting with new information. As with Zembylas's learning and my own example of the demand for ethical consumption, responses should not pigeonhole people into predetermined roles. Their reasonable responses (reflecting their lived reality) should not be negated, but should be explored, appraised (or naturalised) and placed within a framework of responses. This allows the student to acknowledge, appreciate and understand their perspective and then accept that others may have different opinions and values.

Concluding thoughts

This chapter began with a discussion of how emotion in the social studies classroom is often acknowledged but not well understood. Theorists such as Ahmed and Zembylas are exposing the dynamics of the individual, social/relational and contextual intersections of emotions that occur as we teach value-laden topics. For social studies teachers, a greater awareness of these dynamics in our classrooms will better equip us when considering how to broach sensitive or controversial topics and social action. From this mapping of what is potentially going on, I presented three pedagogical complexities and three potential risks to alert teachers to how pedagogical approaches are the key to ensuring emotions are positively acknowledged in social studies. These include accepting that the power of the teacher is less about directing or controlling emotions and more about acknowledging and accepting them as the lived reality learners bring to the classroom. Working with, not against, emotions may produce greater learning.

Todd (2009) argues that unless we face our humanity we are only skimming the surface, and social issues and taking social action will remain a theoretical undertaking and not part of students' lived realities. In our aims as educators the learning outcomes may need to be reprioritised. When our learners think about their social studies classrooms, hopefully they see them as places in which their feelings, thoughts and opinions are heard, valued and identified positively. Taking Zembylas's learning point, a universal code of ethics should not be assumed nor desired. Instead, welcoming and yet challenging all positions encourages critical thinking rather than silent assent to the teacher's desires.

Once learners are affirmed for their own reality, they can start to see themselves as contributing members of society, not only with ideas and opinions but with the confidence to entertain other ideas and perspectives. Providing an environment in which learners can discuss and agonise over ethical dilemmas and bring their emotions and lived experience into the classroom is part of developing their emotional response to difference. Exploring *why* they hold particular views is an integral part of the social studies lesson. This reflexivity then becomes an integral part of the overall goal: to create active, discerning citizens who are enabled to think and act justly, not just within our classrooms but in their everyday realities.

Reflective questions

- Reflect on a time when emotions might have been 'running high' in a social studies lesson. Consider how this situation came about and what were the outcomes? Would you have responded differently another time?

- What are the risks of focusing too much on emotions?
- Are there any risks associated with ignoring emotions?
- How has this chapter made you more aware of emotions within the social studies classroom?

References

Ahmed, S. (2004). Collective feelings, or, the impressions left by others. *Theory Culture Society, 21*(2), 25–42. doi: 10.1177/0263276404042133.

Aitken, G., & Sinnema, C. (2008). *Effective pedagogy in social sciences / Tikanga ā iwi: Best evidence synthesis iteration.* Wellington: Ministry of Education.

Baum, R. (1996). "What have I learned to feel": The pedagogical emotions of Holocaust education. *College Literature, 23*(3), 44–57.

Boler, M. (1999). *Feeling power: Emotion and education.* New York, NY: Routledge.

Evans, R. W., Avery, P. G., & Pederson, P. V. (1999). Taboo topics: Cultural restraint on teaching social issues. *The Social Studies, 90*(5), 218–224. doi: 10.1080/00377999909602419.

Hibbert, S., Smith, A., Davies, A., & Ireland, F. (2007). Guilt appeals: Persuasion knowledge & charitable giving. *Psychology and Marketing, 24*(8), 723–742.

Keown, P. (1998). Values and social action: Doing the hard bits. In P. Benson & R. Openshaw (Eds.), *New horizons for New Zealand social studies* (pp. 137–159). Palmerston North: ERDC Press.

Lindquist, J. (2004). Class affects, classroom affectations: Working through the paradoxes of strategic empathy. *College English, 67*(2), 187–209.

Milligan, A. (2014). *Transcending the ethically silent space of New Zealand's social studies curriculum.* Unpublished doctoral thesis, Victoria University of Wellington.

Seu, B. (2010). 'Doing denial': Audience reaction to human rights appeals. *Discourse and Society, 21*(4), 438–457.

Sheppard, M., Katz, D., & Grosland, T. (2015). Conceptualizing emotions in social studies education. *Theory & Research in Social Education, Citizenship and Social Justice, 43*(2), 147–178. doi: 10.1080/00933104.2015.1034391.

Tallon, R. (2012). Emotion and agency within NGO development education: What is at work and what is at stake in the classroom? *International Journal of Development Education and Global Learning, 4*(2), 5–22.

Tallon, R. (2013). *What do young people think of development?: An exploration into the meanings young people make from NGO media*. Unpublished doctoral thesis, Victoria University of Wellington.

Thrift, N. (2004). Intensities of feeling: Towards a spatial politics of affect. *Geografiska Annaler: Series B, Human Geography, 86*(1), 57–78.

Todd, S. (2009). *Towards an imperfect education: Facing humanity, rethinking cosmopolitanism*. Boulder, CO: Paradigm.

Wood, B. E. (2007). Conflict, controversy, and complexity: Avoiding the 'slippery stuff' in social studies. *Critical Literacy: Theories and Practices, 1*(2), 42–49.

Wood, B. E. (2015). Freedom or coercion?: Citizenship education policies and the politics of affect. In P. Kraftl & M. Blazek (Eds.), *Children's emotions in policy and practice: Mapping and making spaces of childhood* (pp. 259–273). London Palgrave Macmillan.

Wood, B. E., & Taylor, R. M (2016). Caring citizens: Emotional engagement and social action in educational settings in New Zealand. In P. Horton & M. Pyer (Eds.), *Children, young people and care*. Routledge Spaces of Childhood and Youth Series. Abingdon, UK: Routledge

Zembylas, M. (2007). Emotional ecology: The intersection of emotional knowledge and pedagogical content knowledge in teaching. *Teaching and Teacher Education, 23*(4), 355–367.

Zembylas, M. (2012). Pedagogies of strategic empathy: Navigating through the emotional complexities of anti-racism in higher education. *Teaching in Higher Education, 17*(2), 113–125.

Chapter 7 Rethinking literacies in social studies for future-facing young citizens

Philippa Hunter

Key points

- Social studies provides rich opportunities for multi-literacy learning.
- Four types of literacies are promoted through effective social studies: conceptual understandings, responsiveness to diverse cultural contexts and linguistic diversity, use of multimedia and digital technologies, and critical literacy.
- Multi-literacies deepen and expand learning in social studies.

Introduction

While imagining the future lives of young citizens, teachers face the challenge of how to "balance the recognition of change with the recognition of continuity" (Gilbert, 2004, p. 202). Recent cross-curriculum shifts towards language and literacies highlight students' experiences, diversity and learning preferences. This 'linguistic turn' prompts the chapter's focus of social studies literacies that are already embodied in curriculum policy 'speak' and the nature, purpose and methodology of social inquiry. Four interconnected groupings of literacies are proposed to enhance social inquiry. Social studies students are seen as: (i) conceptually aware and engaged meaning-makers, (ii) responsive to diverse cultural contexts and linguistic diversity, (iii) active users of multimedia and digital technologies, and (iv) critically literate and future facing.

The literacies are conceived as active processes that align with national curriculum policy decisions, principles and initiatives that scaffold social studies pedagogical approaches. In promoting pedagogical shifts, the nature of literacies for future-facing young citizens is discussed, and reflective questions are provided for ongoing conversations.

Social sciences policy and curriculum visions

The Social Sciences learning area is centrally positioned in *The New Zealand Curriculum* (*NZC*) (Ministry of Education, 2007). Its socio-cultural approach to learning and thinking focuses on human ways of knowing situated in real-life social and cultural contexts. Social studies teaching and learning relate to understanding "how societies work", and to people's participation in society as "critical, active, informed, and responsible citizens" (p. 30). This aligns with the aim of *Te Marautanga o Aotearoa* (Ministry of Education, 2008) for students' effective and positive participation in the Māori community and global world. *Te Marautanga* supports students to critically examine human social behaviour to "gain an understanding of their world" and examine "ways people meet their physical, social, emotional and spiritual needs" (Ministry of Education, 2012b, p. 19). As the core subject of the social sciences, social studies spans Years 1–13 and is viewed as reflecting the interdisciplinary possibilities of the social sciences (Barr, Graham, Hunter, Keown, & McGee, 1997; Mutch, Hunter, Milligan, Openshaw, & Siteine, 2009). Social studies encourages young people to generate ideas about human social behaviour and embrace changing ways of knowing, such as technology, global connectedness, shifting boundaries, social issues, social justice, and engagement with cultural and linguistic diversity.

Expanding thinking: Social studies' multi-literacies

Social studies' critical place and purpose in the curriculum promotes inclusive pedagogy authentic to the lives of peoples and communities who shape, and who in turn are shaped by, social processes (Ministry of Education, 2007, p. 8). Power relations that embed historical and cultural practices also shape students' informal learning and their literacy practices. In supporting students to meet the *NZC* vision of confident, connected, actively involved and lifelong learners, social studies must be responsive to rapid social change. Multiple literacies are proposed for changing times and within life worlds (Hung, 2011; Kemmis, 2001). The notion of *life worlds* refers to viewing life and society from participants' experiences and perspectives. This means a rethinking of social studies literacy (making meaning) that involves more than reading, writing, understanding texts, communicating knowledge and ideas, and listening and reading critically.[1]

The idea of multidimensional literacy is not new. In 1996 the New London Group of educational researchers aimed to make teaching and learning more inclusive of cultural, linguistic, communicative and technological diversity. The group developed a pedagogy of multi-literacies to respond to changes as a result of new technologies and globalisation that were affecting society (New London Group, 1996). In subsequent publications (Cope & Kalantzis, 2000; Kalantzis & Cope, 2012), multi-literacies and social futures have been theorised as meaning-making in different cultural, social or domain-specific contexts. Kalantzis, Cope, Chan and Dalley-Trim (2016) discuss multi-literacies in terms of new information, and communications as multimodal, whereby written and linguistic modes of meaning interface with oral, visual, audio, gestural, tactile and spatial meaning-making:

> There are … many literacies and these vary according to cultural
> context, social purpose, life experience, personal interest, knowledge
> base and so on. The key is not learning to communicate in the
> one, right way, but how to negotiate these differences in meaning.
> (Kalantzis et al., newlearningonline.com/literacies).

Students' understanding of and communication of identity roles, including those of *citizen* for contemporary and future times, are a critical focus of social studies education and social literacy. To be socially literate involves being able to respond to, and use, an expansion of

---

1   See http://www.minedu.govt.nzliteracyonline for an example of how this is
    conceived in the *NZC*.

symbolic systems (visual images, multimedia, digital technologies) that represent the changing worlds and social diversity lived in and moved across (Boyd & Brock, 2015; Bull & Anstey, 2010). In what follows four literacy groupings are conceived as a coherent system of interconnected active social studies processes, whereby students as members of social and cultural groups are encouraged to engage in understanding and voicing something of their social futures.

(i) Students as conceptually aware and engaged meaning makers

Each learning area in the *NZC* has a statement that explains what it is about, why it is an area for study and how it is structured. The learning areas are shaped by disciplinary conventions, language and linguistic variation that shape ways of knowing. The Social Sciences learning area's core social studies might be understood as a rich cultural site in the national curriculum. Social studies' inter-related and integrated disciplinary knowledge and awareness (social, cultural, political, economic, historical, environmental, etc.) and its methodology of using social inquiry skills processes (inquiry, values and perspectives, social decision making, reflection and evaluation) are unique in the curriculum. The socially constructed subject social studies might be viewed as having a culture in the national schooling curriculum. It has a history, traditions, disciplinary antecedents, and specialist language and vocabulary. Students of all ages are encouraged to generate ideas and apply their understanding across a range of social contexts in past, present and possible future settings.

As Chapter 1 argued, concepts are ideas that are embodied in the cultures and language systems of social worlds. When referring to concepts of leadership (e.g. leader, queen, fa'amatai, mayor, rangatira, politician, government, status, power, authority), we describe, interpret, explain and evaluate ideas about our many life worlds. Because concepts are tools for thinking, they rely on the interpretation of language. No concept has a fixed and universally agreed definition. Rather, there are cultural and shared meanings for concepts. Thus, working with concepts and ideas is not about the transmission of facts and/or information. Rather, it is about developing social knowledge and understanding, and engaging students in learning. Conceptual literacy explored in depth connects students' prior experiences to engage with new ideas and current issues in deep thinking and authentic real-life contexts (Hung, 2011; Hunter & Farthing, 2008; National Council for the Social Studies, n.d.).

The *Effective Pedagogy in Social Sciences / Tikanga ā Iwi: Best Evidence Synthesis Iteration* (Aitken & Sinnema, 2008, p. 230) noted the limited research literature about students' conceptual development in New Zealand. The *Building Conceptual Understandings in the Social Sciences* books support teachers to focus on conceptual learning by offering guidance for directed instruction, graphical tools, contextual examples, recognition and reinforcement of vocabulary (Ministry of Education, 2009a, 2012a). Smart teachers seek evidence of how students construct, apply and defend conceptual understanding in their learning.

Hattie's (2009) research about visible learning—"seeing through the eyes of students and students seeing teaching as the key to their learning" (p. 33)—resonates here. In a social studies learning story, *Improving Pasifika Students' Conceptual Understandings of Government* (Ministry of Education, 2009b), Ana, a deputy principal, worked with a Year 10 class to address the issue of her students "struggling to make connections between their social studies learning and the different worlds they experienced at home, church and with their peers" (p. 2). She planned an intervention focusing on students' conceptual understanding of *systems of government* and the language of *government*. Her evidence-based strategies included: vocabulary and key concepts, pictures or diagrams showing a system of government, and concept circles to describe relationships between words and ideas. Through an inquiry approach as a community of learners, students were encouraged to draw on their life worlds, use language-learning strategies to build conceptual understanding, and communicate diverse cultural ways of knowing.

Identifying *representation* of meaning is a key aspect of working conceptually in social studies. Teachers and students work with multiple modes of representation in social studies, including primary and secondary texts, maps, graphics, statistics, images, interactive and digital modes, artefacts, waiata, simulation games, and storying. Once sourced, modes of information need to be read, heard, analysed, interpreted and critiqued to make meaning. All modes of representation embed and/or indicate concepts and ideas to be identified, examined, interpreted and made sense of through perspectival lenses, values and beliefs. Students who are exposed to a range of modes of representation in social inquiry engage with the *NZC* key competency of *using language, symbols and texts*. This is a critical competency in terms of ways of researching and communicating evidence of thinking in social studies.

Representation in social studies generally indicates something of the disciplinary codes through which knowledge is expressed. As students move into the senior secondary school, the modes of representation become increasingly sophisticated and the demands of disciplinary knowledge and conceptual literacy become greater. Shanahan (2012), a scholar of middle and high school disciplinary literacy, comments that it is unusual for teachers "to help students understand the particular discipline in which they are studying as a frame for reading and learning" (p. 87). Yet she believes this is a crucial element that is missing in instruction: "Teachers should (1) show students appropriate uses of cross-disciplinary strategies and (2) teach them discipline-specific strategies" (p. 88). Social sciences' disciplinary literacy is not about teaching a body of unquestioned facts. Given the opportunity, students' critical capacities and open-mindedness are encouraged (Ochoa-Becker, 2007). Teachers' pedagogical content knowledge of conceptual literacy is critical for assisting students' engagement and early understanding of the ways in which knowledge and meaning are constructed (see also Chapter 3).

(ii) Students who are responsive to diverse cultural contexts and linguistic diversity

Given that social studies is conceptually based and "trade in ideas and representations" (Pearson, 2005, p. 11), it does not have a monopoly on culture, identity or diversity. However, its curriculum purpose is to enable students to "better understand, participate in, and contribute" (Ministry of Education, 2007, p. 30) to the communities in which they live and work. In Aotearoa New Zealand this involves indigenous Māori culture, te reo Māori me ōna tikanga, tribal histories, and bicultural perspectives of history. The *NZC* principles of *Treaty of Waitangi*, *cultural diversity* and *inclusion* (Ministry of Education, 2007, p. 9) are of particular importance to social studies/sciences pedagogies for understanding Māori and Pākehā as full Treaty partners, as a blueprint for intercultural relations, and for valuing diversity as found in cultures, languages and heritages.

Students' responsiveness to diverse cultural contexts and linguistic diversity constitutes meaning making (literacy) in social studies. In the summary of *The Māori Education Strategy: Ka Hikitia: Accelerating Success 2013–2017* (Ministry of Education, 2013), guiding principles are established for Māori students that align with the nature and purpose of social studies pedagogy. These principles emphasise the Treaty of Waitangi, the Māori potential approach, ako, identity, language and culture, and productive partnerships. The *Te Marautanga o Aotearoa* graduate profile (Te āhua ā tātou ākonga) (Ministry of Education, 2012c) for Māori-medium learning focuses on high levels of educational and sociocultural success, a wide range of life skills, and career choices. Likewise, the policy of *Tātaiako: Cultural Competencies for Teachers of Māori Learners* (Ministry of Education, 2011) endorses "genuine, productive relationships among teachers and their Māori students, whānau, iwi, and wider communities" (p. 3). In the foreword to *Tātaiako*, Sharples queries, "How much do the teachers know of their students' history, tikanga, and worldview—and how is this reflected in the classroom curriculum and environment?" (p. 3). This question is critically pertinent to social studies, whereby teacher' understanding of the dimensions of wānanga, whanaungatanga, manaakitanga, tangata whenuatanga and ako[2] promote respectful relationships with students. The development of inquiry into culturally appropriate and responsive contexts for learning promotes and affirms Māori beliefs, language and culture, and social studies must surely take a lead here.

As a situated practice, social studies focuses on students' real lives, concerns and preferences. This involves identifying and rejecting deficit thinking (Bishop & Berryman, 2009) and racist and/or sexist attitudes and language. Forward-thinking social studies teachers and students are responsive to the effects of Aotearoa New Zealand's increasingly diverse cultures and identities. The Royal Society of New Zealand's *Our Futures: Te Pae Tāwhiti* census findings of 2013 on diversity show

---

2   Refer to *Tātaiako: Cultural competencies for teachers of Māori learners* (Ministry of Education, 2011) for an explanation of these concepts. The cultural competencies also link to the Graduating Teacher Standards and Registered Teacher Criteria.

that New Zealand is "increasingly a country with multiple cultural identities and values" (Royal Society of NZ, 2013, p. 3) and that one in four people living in New Zealand in 2013 were born outside New Zealand (p. 4). The report states:

> The most important example of 'diversity' may be in the range of ideas about what is represented and what is valued. A longstanding and deep-seated desire on behalf of the majority community to identify as New Zealanders with a single set of values and practices will be even less apt than in the past. (p. 8)

Consequently, teachers need to know their students and address learning needs through identity work and voicing selves, and encouraging and modelling sensitivity to cultural knowledges and symbolic systems of cultural and linguistic diversity. The Pasifika Education Plan's vision (Ministry of Education, 2012a) is to see every Pasifika learner in schooling "participating, engaging and achieving in education, secure in their identities, languages and cultures and contributing fully to Aotearoa New Zealand's social, cultural and economic wellbeing" (p. 2). Social studies in the national curriculum has a responsibility to ensure students are engaged in learning about the diverse cultural processes and practices of Pasifika communities and beyond.

Resources help to enliven literacies of cultural responsiveness. *The New Zealand Pacific Picture Books Collection* (National Library of New Zealand, 2012) offers picture format books in English, Māori and Pasifika languages. Teacher guidance in this initiative indicates curriculum learning levels, cultural information, context and storying. Another enabling resource for student' voice is the *Living Heritage: Tikanga Tuku Iho* online bilingual initiative (National Library of New Zealand, n.d.).

Students as storytellers and investigators collaborate to write and publish on the web. Recent online stories include Niue Primary School's *Fofoga he Atu Pulapulaola ha Niue*; Moerewa School's Years 1–8 students' *Moerewa Stories*, and Wellington High School's Year 9 students' *Personal Migration Stories*. Students' views of New Zealand and Pacific Island heritages are communicated through their real-life experiences and as active users of multimedia and digital technologies. Engaging students of all ages with traditions and legacies of past-to-present contexts by using future-oriented technologies promotes rich opportunities for student voice, identity work and confidence building.

(iii) Students as active users of multimedia and digital technologies

Meaning-making in social studies is expanded by combining oral, reading and written language with visual, audio and spatial modes of information and communication technology (ICT). Public access online sites with interactive tools useful for social studies inquiry include *Te Ara Encyclopedia of New Zealand, Statistics New Zealand, Heritage New Zealand: Pouhere Taonga, DigitalNZ: A-Tihi o Aotearoa,* and the *Museum of New Zealand: Te Papa Tongarewa* (see the website list at the end of the chapter). The fast-evolving multimedia dimension of social studies involves Web 2.0[3] user-generated tools, digital technologies and interactive modes of ICT to support e-pedagogy. Students draw on multiple literacies and competencies that include the language of popular culture and the immediacy of social media to 'do' literacy, as the learning focus shifts from *what* to *how*. Accordingly, students are encouraged to act as agentive "producers" (Goldfarb, 2002) of their social studies learning, with opportunities to inquire and share findings in novel ways through exploration that has been referred to as active design of social futures (Cope & Kalantzis, 2000).

Interactive websites provide rich media for ICT supported e-pedagogy. The international programme Shared Histories: Mémoires Héritées: Histoire Partagée[4] is an example of this. The site raises awareness of the contribution of the New Zealand Division who fought on the Western Front during World War I, and reflects the wider historical context and contributions of the ANZAC. Students of Pacific-French territories—New Caledonia, French Polynesia and Wallis and Futuna—also participate in the programme. Through inquiry, students design their special way to commemorate shared histories and learn from engaging in both French and English languages through forum discussions and online conferencing.

A further example of the use of multimedia is found on LEARNZ

---

3 Web 2.0 digital tools support user-generated online interactivity, user-generated content, and social networking.

4 http://www.sharedhistories.com/

Virtual Field Trips for New Zealand Schools, which promotes active social studies e-pedagogy supported by ICT.[5] A virtual field trip, *Geohazards*, enables students to enter and explore e-learning environments and overcome barriers of distance and time. For social studies this field trip includes a range of 'up to the mark' technologies—videos, simulation games, interactive maps and graphics, and audio conferencing. Through social inquiry skills processes, students think creatively and critically about what they are learning.

(iv) Students as critically literate and future facing

Social studies education has a key part to play in equipping students to be critically literate and future-facing thinkers and citizens. Critical literacy involves student questioning of the purpose and contexts of social learning, particularly in the senior curriculum as social inquiry contexts become increasingly sophisticated. Questioning in social studies engages students' ideas and beliefs, personal voice and identity construction. The assumptions that students may hold are open for review and disturbance.

Awareness of what knowledge counts and why, and the ways in which knowledge is constructed, becomes a power(ful) dimension of pedagogy. Critical approaches engage students politically, in the sense that they become aware of the ways in which power relations (Lewison, Flint, & Van Sluys, 2002) play out in contexts and settings for study, and how they are represented in multimedia (e.g. Who is represented? Who is misrepresented? Whose perspectives? Whose values? Who has the authority? Whose voice is dominant? What/who is missing?). Social inquiry skills processes of *inquiry, values and perspectives, social decision-making*, and *evaluation and reflection* align with critical literacy. Whether social inquiry is teacher guided or student generated, these processes aim for active critical engagement "with societal issues" (Ministry of Education, 2007, p. 30).

In a curriculum story (Ministry of Education, 2010), Anne, a social sciences curriculum leader, discusses a Year 10 social studies programme at Edgecumbe College. Students join her to explain how their programme, Te Ao Whanui—Local Participation and Global

---

5 http://www.learnz.org.nz.

Confidence, supported them as autonomous learners, contributors to society and global participants. Students acquired relevant knowledge, skills and values to enable them to participate and act in shaping their preferred future for a more peaceful, equitable, just and ecologically sustainable world. The students brought critical literacy skills to thinking about social issues, social change, conflict and human rights. The programme involved identity construction, leadership opportunities, problem solving and reflection on 21st century challenges and citizenship. Students communicated purposefully by using ITC tools and by maintaining e-portfolios.

Engagement with sociopolitical issues prompts students' thinking about social justice, possible action and ethics as young citizens (Hess, 2014). Of necessity, critical literacy for future-oriented social education involves accessing and interpreting media representation. This means developing an awareness of, and questioning, political and economic agendas when researching social issues. The National Council for the Social Studies (2009) signals the importance of media literacy in preparing citizens for democratic life:

> Social studies educators should provide young people with the
> awareness and abilities to critically question and create new media
> and technology, and the digital, democratic experiences, necessary to
> become active participants in the shaping of democracy. (p. 2)

Media literacy is an aspect of critical literacy within social inquiry. Although students need to be informed about their life worlds, they also need to critique the media they access through ICT and understand *what* they are viewing, listening to, reading and interacting with, and *why*. As multi-literate decision makers and citizens in the making, students will take these skills and understandings into their future lives.

Multidimensional literacies and social studies pedagogy

Multidimensional social studies literacies align with the *NZC's* principles and social inquiry methodology. They also align with the *NZC* key competencies, viewed as analogous to social inquiry, as they embed inquiry skills, values exploration and perspectives thinking, social decision making, and attitudes and dispositions (Hunter, 2005, 2009). In particular, the key competencies of *thinking* and *using language, symbols and texts* embody, through pedagogy, the four literacy groupings. The *Best Evidence Synthesis* that supports pedagogy through *connection, alignment, community* and *interest* (Aitken & Sinnema, 2008) also provides a framework that aligns with the rethinking of multidimensional literacies.

Social studies 'plays out' through compelling real-life contexts for learning, where purpose is transparent and students are encouraged to think about *what, how* and *why* they are learning, and what this learning means in terms of their agency as young citizens. Pedagogy must embrace the rapidly changing worlds / life worlds that students inhabit as well as their curiosity, interests and concerns. Teacher agency (positive or negative) is power(ful). Accordingly, as teachers we need to critically reflect on our values systems, perspectives and contextual preferences, because our decisions influence students' educational socialisation. The valuing of students' cultures, languages and diverse experiences supports the power of collaboration and participation. By closely observing learning, and by listening to students' questions, assumptions and social concerns (Hunter & Farthing, 2009), we become aware of issues of access to ways of knowing, stereotypes, clichés and opportunities for critical thinking.

Final thoughts

The multidimensional literacies have been discussed in light of the social studies curriculum's responsibility to support students as future-facing young citizens able to contribute to and participate in their multiple social worlds. In their research about New Zealand-focused future-oriented pedagogy, Bolstad and Gilbert (2012) identify future trends for pedagogy that include personalised learning, addressing the needs of diverse learners, and rethinking teachers' and learners' roles. The identification of themes of diversity, coherence and connectedness resonate with the literacies I have discussed in this chapter. Future trends in teaching and learning must, however, take into account the fast-evolving changes and issues that confront Aotearoa New Zealand society and global settings in the *now*. Indigenous world views and cross-cultural perspectives are prompting a rethinking of citizenship as primarily a sociopolitical identity tied to the nation state.

Multi-literacies assist in redefining ideas about citizenship and the ways citizenship might be practised in the future. Discourses of citizenship include digital technologies for cultural activities and critical thinking skills in cyberspace. International and globalising processes also shape the discourses about what it means to be a global citizen. The current overlapping web of wars and political and sectarian repression in the world has forced millions of people to seek refuge and asylum by undertaking perilous journeys across hostile borders to and through Europe. As a global humanitarian crisis, citizens of Aotearoa New Zealand have been challenged to reflect on, and act on, their moral and legal duty to protect refugees and asylum seekers as world citizens. A closer engagement with multidimensional literacies such as conceptual awareness, responsiveness to cultural and linguistic diversity and the use of multimedia and digital technologies and critical literacy may encourage students to think and act beyond the practice of personally responsible citizenship, to participatory and justice-oriented citizenship (Bolstad, 2012) as reflexive young citizens.

Reflective questions

- What rethinking of social studies pedagogy is needed to embrace the multi-dimensional literacies?
- How do the literacy groupings discussed embed social studies' pedagogical intent and impact?
- How do multi-literacies in social studies connect young citizens with possible futures?
- How might multi-literacies in social studies influence ideas about and practices of citizenship?

References

Aitken, G., & Sinnema, C. (2008). *Effective pedagogy in social sciences / Tikanga ā iwi: Best evidence synthesis iteration.* Wellington: Learning Media.

Barr, H., Graham, J., Hunter, P., Keown, P., & McGee, J. (1997). *A position paper: Social studies in the New Zealand school curriculum.* Hamilton: University of Waikato.

Bishop, R., & Berryman, M. (2009). The Te Kotahitanga effective teaching profile. *set: Research Information for Teachers, 2,* 27–33.

Bolstad, R. (2012). *Participating and contributing? The role of school and community in supporting civic and citizenship education: NZ results from the ICCS Study*. Retrieved from: http://www.nzcer.org.nz/system/files/ Participating-and-Contributing-The-Role-of-School-and-Community.pdf

Bolstad, R., & Gilbert, J., with McDowall, J., Bull, A., Boyd, S., & Hipkins, R. (2012). *Supporting future-oriented learning and teaching: A New Zealand perspective: Report to the Ministry of Education*. Wellington: Ministry of Education.

Boyd, F., & Brock, C. (2015). *Social diversity within multiliteracies: Complexity in teaching and learning*. Abingdon Oxon: Routledge.

Bull, G., & Anstey, M. (2010). *Evolving pedagogies: Reading and writing in a multimodal world*. Carlton Sth, Victoria: Curriculum Press.

Cope, B., & Kalantzis, M. (2000). (Eds). *Multiliteracies: Literacy learning and the design of social futures*. London, UK: Routledge.

Gilbert, R. (2004). (Ed.). *Studying society and environment: A guide for teachers*. Melbourne, Victoria: Thomson.

Goldfarb, B. (2002). *Visual pedagogy: Media cultures in and beyond the classroom*. Durham, NC: Duke University Press.

Hattie, J. (2009). *Visible learning: A synthesis of meta-analyses relating to achievement*. Abingdon, Oxon: Routledge.

Hess, D. (2014). *The political classroom: Evidence and ethics in democratic classrooms*. New York, NY: Routledge.

Hung, R. (2011). Citizenship with/in or without lifeworld?: A critical review of the contemporary perspectives of citizenship. *Policy Futures in Education*, *9*(2), 172–182. Retrieved from http://www.co.uk/PFIE.

Hunter, P. (2005). *Essential skills, key competencies, and the social sciences: Tikanga ā iwi learning area in the New Zealand curriculum*. Report commissioned by the Ministry of Education.

Hunter, P. (2009, September). *Key competencies and social inquiry in the New Zealand curriculum: A way forward for authentic pedagogies*. Paper presented at the Social Sciences Conference 2009 (SocCon09), Christchurch, New Zealand.

Hunter, P., & Farthing, B. (2008). Students think history and teachers learn. *set: Research Information for Teachers*, *1*, 15–24.

Hunter, P., & Farthing, B. (2009). History students voice their thinking: An opening for professional conversations. *set: Research Information for Teachers*, *3,* 52–59.

Kalantzis, M., & Cope, B. (2012). *Literacies*. Cambridge, UK: Cambridge University Press.

Kalantzis, M., Cope, B., Chan, E., & Dalley-Trim, L. (2016). *Literacies* (2nd ed). Cambridge, UK: Cambridge University Press. newlearningonline.com/literacies.

Kemmis, S. (2001). Exploring the relevance of critical theory for action research: Emancipatory action research in the footsteps of Jurgen Habermas. In P. Reason & H. Bradbury (Eds.), *Handbook of action research* (pp. 94–105). Thousand Oaks, CA: Sage.

Lewison, M., Flint, A., & Van Sluys, K. (2002). Taking on critical literacy: The journey of newcomers and novices. *Language Arts, 79*, 382–392.

Ministry of Education. (2007). *The New Zealand curriculum*. Wellington: Learning Media.

Ministry of Education. (2008). *Te marautanga o Aotearoa*. Wellington: Learning Media.

Ministry of Education. (2009a.) *Approaches to building conceptual understandings: Building conceptual understandings in the social sciences*. Wellington: Learning Media.

Ministry of Education. (2009b). *Teachers as learners: Improving outcomes for Maori and Pasifika students through inquiry. Story 1: Improving Pasifika students' conceptual understandings of government*. Retrieved from http://nzcurriculum.tki.org.nz/ Curriculum-stories/ Case-studies/.

Ministry of Education (2010). *Curriculum story: Te ao whanui: Local participation, global confidence*. Retrieved from http://nzcurriculum.tki.org.nz/Curriculum-stories/Media-gallery/Student-voice/Te-Ao-Whanui.

Ministry of Education. (2011). *Tātaiako: Cultural competencies for teachers of Maori learners*. Wellington: Author. Retrieved from http://www.tmoa.tki.org.nz/Te-Marautanga-o-Aotearoa

Ministry of Education. (2012a). *Pasifika education plan 2013–2017*. Wellington: Author. Retrieved from http://www.education.govt.nz/ministry-of-education/overall-strategies-and-policies/pasifika-education-plan-2013-2017/

Ministry of Education. (2012b). *Taking part in economic activities: Building conceptual understandings in the social sciences*. Wellington: Author.

Ministry of Education. (2012c). *Te marautanga o Aotearoa: Whakapākehātanga*. Wellington: Author.

Ministry of Education. (2013). *The Maori education strategy: Ka hikitia— Accelerating success 2013–2017*. Wellington: Author.

Mutch, C., Hunter, P., Milligan, A., Openshaw, R., & Siteine, A. (2009, August). *Understanding the social sciences as a learning area: A position paper.* Retrieved from http://nzcurriculum.tki.org.nz/curriculum-resources/nzc-resource.bank/social.sciences/ key-resources.

National Council for the Social Studies. (2009). *Media literacy.* Retrieved from http://www.socialstudies.org/positions/medialiteracy.

National Council for the Social Studies. (n.d.) *A vision of powerful teaching and learning in the social studies: Building social understanding and civic efficacy.* Retrieved from http://www.socialstudies.org.

National Library of New Zealand. (2012). *The New Zealand Pacific picture books collection.* Retrieved from http://schools.natlib.govt.nz/blogs/create-readers/12-10/new-zealand-pacific-picture-books-collection.

National Library of New Zealand. (n.d.). *Living heritage: Tikanga tuku iho.* Retrieved from http://www.livingheritage.org.nz.

New London Group. (1996). A pedagogy of multiliteracies: Designing social futures. *Harvard Educational Review, 66*(1), 60–92.

Ochoa-Becker, A. (2007). *Democratic education for social studies: An issues-centered decision making curriculum.* New York, NY: Information Age Publishing.

Pearson, D. (2005). Citizenship, identity and belonging: Addressing the mythologies of the unitary nation state in Aotearoa/New Zealand. In J. Liu, T. McCreanor, & T. Teaiwa (Eds.), *New Zealand identities: Departures and destinations* (pp. 21–37). Wellington: Victoria University Press.

Royal Society of New Zealand. (2013). *Our futures: Te pae tāwhiti.* Retrieved from http://assets.royalsociety.org.nz/media/2014/08/Our-Futures-report-web-with-references.pdf.

Shanahan, C. (2012). How disciplinary experts read. In T. Jetton & C. Shanahan (Eds.), *Adolescent literacy in the academic disciplines: General principles and practical strategies* (pp. 69–91). New York, NY: Guildford Press.

Useful websites

DigitalNZ—National Library of New Zealand: http://www.digitalnz.org

Heritage New Zealand: Pouhere Taonga: http://www.heritage.org.nz

Statistics NZ: http://www.stats.govt.nz

Te Ara Enclopedia of New Zealand: http://www.teara.govt.nz/en

The Museum of New Zealand: Te Papa Tongarewa: http://www.tepapa.govt.nz

Chapter 8 How to use assessment to enhance learning in social studies

Rose Atkins and Peter Rawlins

Key points

- Assessment is a critical component of effective learning and teaching in social studies.
- Assessing discipline-specific knowledge and skills, and affective dispositions, can present challenges in social studies, especially in relation to knowing what to assess.
- There are research-led assessment practices that can be used to enhance learning in social studies.
- Students' progress in social studies can be communicated in a learning-oriented manner.

Introduction

A core aim of this book is to outline pedagogical practices that will support students to develop knowledge, skills and dispositions that will empower them to become critically informed citizens, equipped to actively and responsibly shape their social worlds. Assessment is integral to this process, yet teachers in New Zealand say they struggle to know what aspects of students' learning in social studies to assess. In this chapter we outline what effective assessment involves and how it can be used to foster transformative learning in social studies. We look at challenges that teachers face with assessing learning in social studies and ways in which the Ministry of Education's requirements to transparently communicate students' achievements in a progressive manner might be met.

The goal of assessment

Assessment guides teachers' and students' judgements about what is important to learn. It helps students consolidate and demonstrate their learning and can contain messages that influence their perceptions of themselves as learners. Assessment can influence students' self-efficacy, motivation to learn, sense of empowerment, autonomy and ability to develop enduring learning strategies that will help them adapt and respond to new experiences. Assessment is therefore integral to learning and one of the most potent forces affecting students' learning.

For assessment to be effective it needs to make a strong contribution to improving students' learning and teachers' teaching (Wiliam, 2011). This view is clearly conveyed in the purpose statement for assessment in *The New Zealand Curriculum* (*NZC*):

> The primary purpose of assessment is to improve students' learning and teachers' teaching as both student and teacher respond to the information that it provides. (Ministry of Education, 2007, p. 39)

While evidence suggests that effective assessment supports and promotes learning, simply increasing the amount of assessment does not guarantee improved learning. Rather, it is the nature and purpose of the assessment that has the biggest impact on students' learning. Assessment that accounts for students' diverse social, cultural and academic needs and learning contexts has been found to facilitate effective learning in social studies (Aitken & Sinnema, 2008; Atkins, 2010).

What should we be assessing in social studies?

Given that a key goal of learning in social studies is to empower students to develop into active and critically informed citizens, equipped to responsibly shape their social worlds, this needs to be reflected in how their learning is assessed. Recent discipline-based research contends that teachers should be focusing on assessing students' discipline-specific conceptual knowledge, ability to engage in critically reflective social inquiries, and affective dispositions (sense of agency and social empathy) through a cumulative range of constructively aligned and performance-based assessments (Aitken & Sinnema, 2008; Atkins, 2010; Wood & Milligan, 2010). Constructively aligned assessments are linked to learning objectives and teaching programmes—usually based on the *NZC*—so that decisions about future teaching and learning are evidence based (Biggs & Tang, 2011). Performance-based assessments involve students moving beyond traditional written forms of communication in order to apply their emerging knowledge, skills, perspectives and dispositions to 'real-world' contexts.

Although it might appear clear what needs to be assessed in social studies, assessment programmes in New Zealand do not always transparently feature concept-, performance- and values-based assessment tasks (Atkins, 2010; Education Review Office, 2007a, 2007b). The way social studies has been conveyed in national curricula (Department of Education, 1977; Ministry of Education, 1997, 2007), the paucity of discipline-specific assessment tools, and the way in which recent professional learning materials have been disseminated have all contributed to this issue.

Curriculum structure

As discussed in previous chapters, social studies is founded on a tradition of civic literacy and participation (Abbiss, 2011; Aitken, 2005; Barr, 1998). The *NZC*, though entrenched in these traditions, conveys learning in social studies as a non-prescriptive and non-hierarchical body of knowledge, skills and affective attributes. The discipline-specific knowledge is conveyed in four overarching conceptual strands and a series of conceptually based achievement objectives, while the participatory and affective aspects of learning—related to social action and the analysis of multiple perspectives and values—are conveyed through a generalised social inquiry approach. Many achievement objectives mention using a New Zealand context, yet there is little guidance on what groups, locations or time periods should be covered.

Whether the achievement objectives listed in the higher levels of the *NZC* are more conceptually complex than lower-level achievement objectives has been widely debated. For example, what makes the following Level 5 achievement more complex than the Level 3 statement?

> Level 5: Students learn "that people move between places and how this has consequences for the people and the places."

> Level 3: Students learn "how the movement of people affects cultural diversity and interaction in NZ". (Ministry of Education, 2007)

In practice the complexity is often based on how teachers interpret the achievement objectives, the contexts they select and the depth of understanding they expect their students to develop. These judgements are often subjective and based on the teacher's perception of the literacy capabilities, and life experiences, of their students. The non-prescriptive and non-hierarchical nature of the social studies curriculum has been widely critiqued (Aitken, 2005; Aitken & Sinnema, 2008; Atkins, 2010; Milligan, 2006).

When considering assessment, is the lack of prescription and hierarchical structure really an issue? Previous research would suggest that it is. Recent studies have shown that:

- assessment practices and student achievement in social studies vary greatly
- novice teachers feel uncertain about what achievement at different levels looks like
- assessing broad conceptual understanding is more complex than assessing narrow bodies of prescribed content
- students' progress is being reported in an invalid hierarchical manner in some schools.

> (Atkins, 2010; Education Review Office, 2007b; Milligan & Wood, 2010)

As an example of this last point, there are cases where students who have been judged as having a sound knowledge of concepts related to Level 5 achievement objectives are being reported as achieving at a more advanced level than students who have a sound knowledge of concepts related to Level 4 achievement objectives (Atkins, 2010). This type of reporting is invalid because students do not necessarily have to master Level 4 concepts to understand Level 5 concepts in social studies.

Whether future iterations of the social studies curriculum could, or should, have a hierarchical structure is beyond the scope of this discussion. Of more importance to the focus of this chapter is how teachers can assess discipline-specific learning in a way that enhances learning and demonstrates progress—ideas that will be explored in the later part of the chapter.

Assessment guidance

The Ministry of Education's *Assessment Online* page on *Te Kete Ipurangi* (http://assessment.tki.org.nz) and the *NZC* have a lot of good advice on assessment, but they do not contain subject-specific resources or guidance on how to formally assess learning in social studies. A few discipline-specific resources that do so include:

- the social studies exemplars (Ministry of Education, 2004), which demonstrate what quality learning at Levels 1–5 of the previous curriculum (Ministry of Education, 1997) looks like through annotated examples of student work

- the National Education Monitoring Project (NEMP) and National Monitoring Study of Student Achievement reports (e.g. Smith, Crooks, Gilmore, & White, 2009; Ministry of Education, 2015), which outline Year 4 and Year 8 students' attitudes towards, and achievement in, social studies (with some of the NEMP assessment tasks being accessible to teachers)

- the *Building Conceptual Understandings in the Social Sciences* series (e.g. Ministry of Education, 2009), which contains general mentions of assessment under *formative assessment* banners

- the NZQA and Ministry of Education websites[1], which contain exemplars of student work and assessment advice for teachers implementing NCEA-level social studies.

How widely the information in these resources has been read or embedded in current practice is difficult to know. These resources are all available on the web and hard copies of many of them have been sent

---

1   http://www.nzqa.govt.nz/qualifications-standards/qualifications/ncea/
    subjects/social-studies/levels/ and http://ncea.tki.org.nz/Resources-
    for-Internally-Assessed-Achievement-Standards/Social-sciences/
    Social-studies

to schools. Yet Atkins (2010) found that the teachers she interviewed were not using the social studies exemplars to inform their practice, and her recent survey of Year 9 and 10 social studies teachers found that 47 percent of the 464 respondents had *rarely if ever* used ideas from the *Building Conceptual Understandings in the Social Sciences* booklets, 42 percent had *rarely if ever* used NCEA social studies resources, and over 71 percent wanted more guidance on how to assess learning in social studies.

Regardless of challenges like those outlined above, if "the primary purpose of assessment is to improve students' learning and teachers' teaching" in an evidence-informed manner (Ministry of Education, 2007, p. 39), then teachers at all levels of schooling need to understand what the purpose of assessment is and how to foster an *assessment for learning* philosophy in their formal assessment practices.

Recognising the dual purposes of assessment

Assessment is said to have two main purposes: *formative* and *summative*. Assessment that serves a *formative* purpose (called *formative assessment* or *assessment for learning*) aims to elicit information about students' present understanding and performance, to guide teachers and students in co-developing the next steps in learning (Ministry of Education, 2007; Smith, 2010; Wiliam, 2011). Diagnostic assessment (which identifies gaps and patterns of learning strengths and difficulties) is now commonly considered a form of *formative assessment* (e.g. Harlen, 2012). Assessment that serves a *summative* purpose (called *summative assessment* or *assessment of learning*) aims to summarise students' learning at a given point in time. Judgements from summative assessment points are often reported to stakeholders (students, parents, teachers, employers) as marks, grades or statements of what has been learnt.

The shortened versions of these assessment terms have unfortunately led to some confusion (Ussher & Earl, 2010). For example, shortening 'assessment for formative purposes' to 'formative assessment' has resulted in some teachers believing that it is the assessment task that is formative rather than the task being part of a 'process' where the information it generates is used for formative purposes. Using the terms 'formative assessment' and 'summative assessment' can also lead to the belief that an assessment task only has one intended purpose (Ussher & Earl, 2010). In reality, an assessment task can generate information that can be used for multiple purposes, such as ascertaining present understanding of key concepts, identifying misconceptions, providing evidence of student achievement, and indicating how effective the teaching has been. Accordingly, it is not the assessment instrument that is formative or summative but how and when the information it generates is used. A single assessment task can therefore serve both a formative and a summative purpose (Black, Harrison, Hodgen, Marshall, & Serret, 2011; Harlen, 2012; Taras, 2009). While acknowledging the debate about and variation in how these terms are defined, for readability we will use the shortened versions.

The summative and formative purposes of assessment can at times be in tension with institutional demands. The constant demand to measure and report student achievement means that summative assessment often takes precedence, resulting in limited conscious and documented use of formative assessment processes (Black & Wiliam, 1998; Carless, 2007; Wiliam, Lee, Harrison, & Black, 2004). Given that formative assessment has the greatest potential for positively influencing future learning, it is essential that all teachers understand how to work with students to use assessment to guide future learning (Rawlins & Leach, 2014). Improving assessment literacy and students' autonomy in learning have been key features of recent assessment policies in New Zealand (Ministry of Education, 2011).

Using assessment to promote learning in social studies

Assessment practices that can promote learning involve *informal*, everyday, 'in the moment' assessments as well as *formal* assessments that take place at pre-specified times. Teachers therefore need to move beyond simply measuring and reporting students' progress against predetermined assessment criteria to facilitate student engagement in assessment. Making the most of formative assessment opportunities can increase students' autonomy and involvement in learning and assessment (Absolum, Flockton, Hattie, Hipkins, & Reid, 2009; Ministry of Education, 2011). Everyday classroom practices, such as feedback, self- and peer assessment, learning-oriented questioning, and concept-based social inquiries, have the potential to: promote student engagement, reveal the knowledge, skills and dispositions that students are developing in social studies, and inform decisions about potential next steps. Ways that each of these four assessment practices can be used to promote learning in social studies are outlined in the numbered sections below.

1. Feedback

Feedback has been identified as having one of the most powerful influences on students' learning and achievement (Hattie & Timperley, 2007). Depending on the particular characteristics of the feedback, this influence can be positive, neutral or negative. As outlined in Table 8.1, *ego-oriented* feedback, for example, tends to concentrate on broader aspects of the learner's dispositions or abilities, while *task-oriented* feedback concentrates on specific aspects of the task and, importantly, what students can do to improve their performance.

Table 8.1: Different forms of feedback

Examples of ego-oriented feedback	"I can see you tried hard on this task."
	"You are good at social studies."
Examples of task-oriented feedback	"You have identified some valid views on this water issue, the *next step* would be to name specific people or groups who hold these views. Then demonstrate how their views align or differ."
	"Great suggestions on how to solve this problem. *You now need to work out which of your suggested actions is most feasible.*"

Task-oriented feedback is potentially the most effective type of feedback because it:

- acknowledges students' progress towards specified learning outcomes
- provides context-specific responses to students' errors and omissions
- sets tangible next steps.

Effective feedback is therefore based on the premise that students' knowledge is partial or incomplete, and mistakes are a normal part of learning. This feedback can be delivered in a variety of forms—individual or whole-class written or verbal comments, marks and grades—from multiple sources—teachers, self and peers—and should answer three questions: Where am I going? How am I going? Where to next? (Hattie & Timperley, 2007, p. 87).

When teachers provide valid and reliable judgements about the quality of students' work, with suggested next-step actions, they may think they have given students effective *formative feedback*. This feedback will not necessarily lead to improvements in learning or performance, however. Many students only look at their grades, thus failing to recognise that their teacher's feedback may provide helpful *formative* signals as to what to do next. In addition, students sometimes do not know what to do with the feedback they receive. The feedback therefore becomes "dangling data" (Sadler, 1989), because it can only become formative when students use it to inform subsequent learning. Students therefore need to be given regular opportunities to learn how to process the feedback they are given (Rawlins & Leach, 2014). For example, the following stem could be used to help students process their teacher's feedback:

> When my teacher says, "You now need to work out which of your suggested actions is most feasible", it means I need to ....

While student engagement in feedback is critical for effective learning to occur, so is their engagement in self- and peer assessment (Wiliam, 2011).

2. Self- and peer assessment

Self- and peer assessment encourage greater student autonomy, because teachers share the responsibility for assessment with students, thus helping them to become 'apprentices in judgement'. For example, the application of criteria to their own and others' work helps students to internalise the criteria. Self- and peer assessment also encourage higher-level thinking skills, such as metacognition. When students monitor their current understanding, they self-regulate, plan what to do next, check the outcomes of strategies they have employed, evaluate, and revise their plans.

Unfortunately, despite evidence that self- and peer assessment are beneficial to students' learning, research has identified that they are not common practice, even among teachers who take assessment seriously. Further, some argue that students cannot be trusted to self- or peer assess accurately (Black, Harrison, Lee, Marshall, & Wiliam, 2003; OECD, 2005; Rawlins & Leach, 2014; Tiknaz & Sutton, 2006).

Stem phrases linked to discipline-specific conceptual knowledge, performance skills, and affective dispositions—as opposed to ego-oriented smiley face charts ☺ ☺ ☹ and stems like "I am confident about …"— can encourage students to engage in robust, task-oriented self- and peer assessment in social studies (see Table 8.2).

Table 8.2: How to promote self- and peer assessment

Examples from a reflective journal task	Theoretical explanation
1. In social studies I have learnt that [insert concept] means … 2. Activities that we have done in class that have helped me understand this big idea are …	All stems in this task promote metacognition through the self-assessment of learning.
3. Perspectives that I know specific people/ groups have expressed towards this concept are … 4. Ways this concept relates to other concepts I've studied are ….	Stems 3 and 4 encourage students to engage in higher-order conceptual thinking because students must explore people's perspectives on the concept and make links to other concepts.
5. To increase my understanding of this concept I need to …	Stem 5 promotes next-step goal setting
Peer feedback: Please comment on the accuracy of their responses and add some additional points or next step suggestions if you can.	This peer feedback stem promotes task-oriented feedback from a peer and higher-order conceptual thinking about the focus concept(s).

Although the examples in Table 8.2 are taken from a written activity, the same sort of questions could be used during oral interactions.

3. Learning-oriented questioning

Questioning is another informal *formative assessment* practice that can help make students' thinking visible. Not all forms of questioning lead to high-quality learning-oriented assessment conversations. Critical in this distinction is whether the information generated from the questions is used to support the teacher's instructional decisions in relation to the next steps in learning.

Traditionally, teachers' questions have often failed to require students to explain or justify their thinking. As a result, teachers commonly fall into the trap of pursuing a 'correct response' and proceeding down a predetermined learning pathway without using the students' answers to inform instructional decisions. Ruiz-Primo and Furtak (2006) have proposed an interactive and learning-oriented questioning framework consisting of four key elements—ESRU (elicit, student, recognise, uses)—to avoid this.

1. The teacher asks a question to *elicit* students' thinking as fully as possible by, for example, inviting students to share their ideas or explain their reasoning.

2. The *student* tries to make their thinking as explicit as possible when responding to the question.

3. The teacher *recognises* or validates the student's response by absorbing it into the ongoing classroom conversation without making an evaluative judgement about its correctness. This could include revoicing or rephrasing the student's response, acknowledging an alternative perspective, or clarifying aspects of the explanation.

4. The teacher *uses* information in a student's response to decide where to direct students' subsequent learning. This direction might have been anticipated by the teacher in their lesson plan, or it may be an unanticipated direction. The critical point is that the next step in the learning sequence is determined by using what the student says. Strategies for using information supplied by students may include: expanding students' thinking with why/how-type questions, comparing and contrasting students' alternative explanations, collaboratively exploring students' ideas, promoting consensus, providing helpful feedback, and helping to relate evidence to explanations (Ruiz-Primo & Furtak, 2006).

Table 8.3: Using ERSU in social studies

Example		Theoretical explanation
Teacher:	How could our class provide aid for people in Nepal affected by the recent earthquake?	**Elicit** ideas about appropriate social actions
Student:	We could bake them some cakes.	**Student** responds
Teacher:	So what you are saying is that we should bake some cakes and send them to Nepal. How would we send the cakes there? (This could be followed by questions like, 'How long would it take for the cakes to get there?' and 'Would they still be fresh?')	**Recognition** of the student's partial understanding of the concept of providing aid and **use** of the student's response to activate more critical thinking on the practicalities of the social actions that have been suggested.

In Table 8.3 the teacher has not made evaluative judgements in their response. If they had immediately asked the class to supply other ideas it could have signalled to students that there were right/wrong answers to the initial question. The opportunity to help students develop a more in-depth understanding of decision-making processes, related to how people respond to crises, could also have been missed.

As with all effective pedagogies, the *using* phase is critical (see example in Table 8.3). As teachers work to make sense of students' responses they must immediately and continuously make decisions about the directions their future teaching needs to move in. These decisions will ultimately determine whether students' existing understanding is developed and their learning needs are met.

4. Concept-based formal assessment tasks

If, as Milligan and Wood (2010) contend, conceptual understanding is a transition point in a student's learning in social studies, assessment tasks that are designed to reveal students' current conceptual understanding can help teachers and students enact the formative potential of their formal assessments. Assessment tasks that provide students with the opportunity to discuss important social studies concepts, draw connections between concepts, apply current concept-based understanding to new contexts and analyse people's perspectives can help students demonstrate more abstract and higher-order conceptual thinking. Concept-based assessment tasks also enable teachers and students to track how subsequent learning is adding to, or changing, current understanding, so that they can adjust future learning and teaching pathways if needed.

The *formative* potential of formal assessment tasks can be increased by:

- constructing open-ended social inquiry tasks that encourage students to explore broad concepts rather than simply recalling atomised content—open-ended tasks can provide students with the opportunity to transfer ideas and actions developed in one real-world context to another, explore multiple perspectives on social issues, actively engage in meaningful personal social actions, and develop a sense of their personal identity (see Table 8.4)

- using stem descriptors from hierarchical taxonomies, such as Bloom (Anderson & Krathwohl, 2001) and SOLO (Biggs & Tang, 2011) (see Table 8.4)

- including self-or peer assessment tasks and/or providing task- and process-oriented feedback comments (see Tables 8.1, 8.2 and 8.5)
- creating marking rubrics that contain descriptors that can be applied to multiple contexts and reveal the sophistication of students' conceptual thinking, participatory citizenship and/or sense of social responsibility (see Table 8.5).

Table 8.4: Identifying the formative potential in formal assessment tasks

Example	Theoretical explanation
1. Explain why people think it is important for NZ to have marine reserves. (Instead of 'How many marine reserves does NZ have?')	This open-ended question encourages students to engage in critical thinking as they explore people's perspectives and the links between concepts like sustainability, scarcity, protection and resources.
2. Evaluate whether having marine reserves is protecting marine environments.	The open-ended nature of task 2 and the 'evaluate' stem require students to engage in abstract thinking as they consider the issue from multiple perspectives.
3. Make a case for establishing a new marine reserve in a chosen location.	Task 3 encourages students to actively engage in a robust social inquiry and potentially generalise from knowledge gained in a context they have studied.

Table 8.5: Flexible concept-based marking rubrics

	Examples: Excerpts from two assessment schedules			
	Working towards	Meets	Exceeds	Vastly exceeds
	the expected depth of thinking about Level 5 concepts	the expected depth of thinking about Level 5 concepts	the expected depth of thinking about Level 5 concepts	the expected depth of thinking about Level 5 concepts
Social studies conceptual understandings in the NZC	The student:			
	Criteria for tasks 1 and 2 of the marine reserve task in Box 8.4			
	defines	describes	compares	evaluates
	what a marine reserve is	why marine reserves are needed	people's perspectives on the need and effectiveness of marine reserves	people's perspectives on the effectiveness of marine reserves
	Criteria for multiple entries in the reflective journaling task in Box 8.2			
	defines	describes	explains	critiques
	a concept	the relationship between the defined concept and a selected context	the relationship between multiple concepts	multiple perspectives on relevant concepts

The internal hierarchy in the assessment schedules in Table 8.5 moves from simple description to complex critique. This structure can enable teachers to report students' progress in relation to a selected level of conceptual understanding from the *NZC* (e.g. Level 5) in a valid and progressive manner.

A concept-based assessment programme therefore has the potential to help teachers to help students engage in broader and deeper conceptual thinking and record learning in a valid and progressive manner.

Reporting learning in a progressive manner

As stated above, assessing transferable conceptual knowledge and discipline-specific performance in social studies provides teachers with the opportunity to report students' learning in a progressive manner. For example, Figure 8.1 illustrates how a Year 9 student's developing conceptual thinking in social studies might be graphically represented.

Figure 8.1: Reporting progress in Year 9 social studies

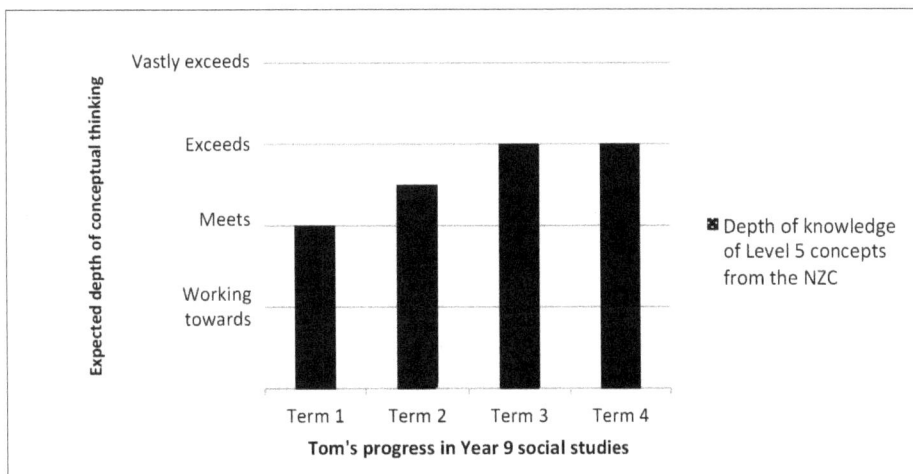

The graph in Figure 8.1 should be supported by a brief narrative statement because the Ministry of Education's expectation is that students' achievements should be reported in plain, jargon-free language that parents, students and other interested stakeholders can easily interpret.

Many schools are currently using NCEA grade descriptors on their junior reports. This has caused some parents to mistakenly think their Year 10 child has gained some NCEA credits (Atkins, 2010), so schools must carefully consider the types of coding scales and narrative descriptors they use on their reports.

Final thoughts

Assessment is an integral component of effective learning in social studies, so teachers need to embed *assessment for learning* principles in their everyday practice. The strategies and practical examples outlined above exemplify ways these principles might operate in a social studies context. Although we have acknowledged that the structure of the current national social studies curriculum does present teachers with challenges in reporting students' learning in a progressive manner, we have offered suggestions for how to validly judge students' learning to inform future learning. The key to maximising the formative potential of assessment in social studies is to critically reflect on the information that your assessments provide and base next-step learning and teaching goals on this information. Only then will assessment begin to foster transformative learning in social studies and empower students to become critically informed citizens able to responsibly shape their future world.

Reflective questions

- What ideas from this chapter seem most pertinent to the way you assess learning? Explain why you chose these ideas.

- What advantages and challenges do assessing students' conceptual understanding in social studies provide?

- Formative assessment is powerful but complex to carry out successfully. What needs to change for it to become more firmly embedded in your role as student teacher, teacher, head of department or syndicate leader?

References

Abbiss, J. (2011). Social sciences in the New Zealand curriculum: Mixed messages. *Curriculum Matters, 7*, 118–137.

Absolum, M., Flockton, L., Hattie, J., Hipkins, R., & Reid, I. (2009). *Directions for assessment in New Zealand*. Retrieved from http://assessment. tki.org.nz/Assessment-in-the-classroom/Assessment-position-papers.

Aitken, G. (2005). The purpose and substance of social studies: Citizenship education possibilities. In P. Benson & R. Openshaw (Eds.), *Towards effective social studies* (pp. 83–110). Palmerston North: Kanuka Grove Press.

Aitken, G., & Sinnema, C. (2008). *Effective pedagogy in social sciences / Tikanga ā iwi: Best evidence synthesis iteration.* Wellington: Ministry of Education.

Anderson, L. W., & Krathwohl, D. R. (2001). *A taxonomy for learning, teaching, and assessing: A revision of Bloom's taxonomy of educational objectives.* New York: Longman.

Atkins, R. A. (2010). *Assessment practices in New Zealand Year 9 and 10 social studies courses: An exploratory case study.* Unpublished master's thesis, Massey University, Palmerston North. Retrieved from http://hdl.handle.net/10179/2216.

Barr, H. (1998). The nature of social studies. In P. Benson & R. Openshaw (Eds.), *New horizons for New Zealand social studies* (pp. 103–120). Palmerston North: ERDC Press.

Biggs, J. B., & Tang, C. (2011). *Teaching for quality learning at university: What the student does* (4th ed.). Maidenhead, UK: McGraw-Hill Education.

Black, P., Harrison, C., Hodgen, J., Marshall, B., & Serret, N. (2011). Can teachers' summative assessments produce dependable results and also enhance classroom learning? *Assessment in Education: Principles, Policy & Practice, 18*(4), 451–469. doi: 10.1080/0969594x.2011.557020.

Black, P., Harrison, C., Lee, C., Marshall, B., & Wiliam, D. (2003). *Assessment for learning: Putting it into practice.* Maidenhead, UK: Open University Press.

Black, P., & Wiliam, D. (1998). Assessment and classroom learning. *Assessment in Education: Principles, Policy & Practice, 5*(1), 7–71. doi: 10.1080/0969595980050102.

Carless, D. (2007). Conceptualizing pre-emptive formative assessment. *Assessment in Education: Principles, Policy & Practice, 14*(2), 171–184. doi: 10.1080/09695940701478412.

Department of Education. (1977). *Social studies syllabus guidelines: Forms 1–4.* Wellington: Author.

Education Review Office. (2007a). *The collection and use of assessment information in schools.* Wellington: Author.

Education Review Office. (2007b). *The teaching of social studies: Good practice.* Wellington: Author.

Harlen, W. (2012). On the relationship between assessment for formative and summative purposes. In J. Gardner (Ed.), *Assessment and learning* (2nd ed., pp. 87–102). London, UK: Sage.

Hattie, J., & Timperley, H. (2007). The power of feedback. *Review of Educational Research, 77*(1), 8–112. doi: 10.3102/003465430298487.

Milligan, A. (2006). *Representing the social world: New Zealand's social studies curriculum change.* Unpublished master's thesis, Victoria University of Wellington, Wellington.

Milligan, A., & Wood, B. E. (2010). Conceptual understandings as transition points: Making sense of a complex social world. *Journal of Curriculum Studies, 42*(4), 487–501. doi: http://dx.doi.org/10.1080/00220270903494287.

Ministry of Education. (1997). *Social studies in the New Zealand curriculum.* Wellington: Learning Media.

Ministry of Education. (2004). *The New Zealand curriculum exemplars: Social studies.* Wellington: Learning Media & the Learning Centre Trust of New Zealand.

Ministry of Education. (2007). *The New Zealand curriculum.* Wellington: Learning Media.

Ministry of Education. (2009). *Building conceptual understandings in the social sciences: Approaches to building conceptual understandings.* Wellington: Learning Media.

Ministry of Education. (2011). *Position paper: Assessment.* Wellington: Learning Media.

Ministry of Education. (2015). *National monitoring study of student achievement: Social studies 2014 overview.* Dunedin: Educational Assessment Research Unit, University of Otago; and Wellington: New Zealand Council for Educational Research.

OECD (Ed.). (2005). *Formative assessment: Improving learning in secondary classrooms.* Paris, France: OECD Publishing.

Rawlins, P., & Leach, L. (2014). Questions in assessment for learning and teaching. In A. M. St George, S. Brown, & J. O'Neill (Eds.), *Facing the big questions in teaching: Purpose, power and learning* (pp. 36–43). Melbourne, VIC: Cengage Learning.

Ruiz-Primo, M., & Furtak, E. (2006). Informal formative assessment and scientific inquiry: Exploring teachers' practices and student learning. *Educational Assessment, 11*(3&4), 205–235.

Sadler, D. R. (1989). Formative assessment and the design of instructional systems. *Instructional Science, 18,* 119–144.

Smith, J., Crooks, T., Gilmore, A., & White, J. (2009). *Social studies: Assessment results 2009.* Dunedin: Educational Assessment Research Unit, University of Otago.

Smith, K. (2010). Assessment: Complex concept and complex practice. *Assessment Matters, 2,* 6–19.

Taras, M. (2009). Summative assessment: The missing link for formative assessment. *Journal of Further and Higher Education, 33*(1), 57–69. doi: 10.1080/03098770802638671.

Tiknaz, Y., & Sutton, A. (2006). Exploring the role of assessment tasks to promote formative assessment in key stage 3 geography: Evidence from twelve teachers. *Assessment in Education: Principles, Policy & Practice, 13*(3), 327–343. doi: 10.1080/09695940601035502.

Ussher, B., & Earl, K. (2010). 'Summative' and 'formative': Confused by the assessment terms? *New Zealand Journal of Teachers' Work, 7*(1), 53–63.

Wiliam, D. (2011). What is assessment for learning? *Studies in Educational Evaluation, 37*(1), 3–14. doi: 10.1016/j.stueduc.2011.03.001.

Wiliam, D., Lee, C., Harrison, C., & Black, P. (2004). Teachers developing assessment for learning: Impact on student achievement. *Assessment in Education: Principles, Policy & Practice, 11*(1), 49–65. doi: 10.1080/0969594042000208994.

Wood, B. E., & Milligan, A. (2010). Possibilities for assessment in social studies: What could we be looking for in student work? *set: Research Information for Teachers, 2,* 17–24.

Conclusion

Nearly 20 years ago, Barr (1998) argued that, among differing definitions for social studies, there are commonly agreed 'twin goals' of social studies learning: to gain greater understandings of society and to develop skills to participate within it. In concluding, we return to two key questions associated with these goals that are addressed by the authors within this book: *What is the nature of knowledge in social studies,* and *How do social studies students learn critical and active citizenry?* In doing so, we draw together many of the themes evident in the chapters of this book, and connect some of the key arguments to wider, ongoing considerations about what counts as knowledge and the type of citizen we wish to create.

What is the nature of knowledge in social studies?

A key premise of this book is that social studies teaching and learning is concept—rather than fact or topic—led. The US educator Taba (1962), whose work has considerably informed New Zealand's social studies curriculum, argued that conceptual approaches provide a more durable and meaningful foundation for teaching and learning than merely memorising large amounts of factual knowledge. This position is particularly elaborated by Jane Abbiss in Chapter 1. She argues that while social studies remains the cause of some confusion, the subject has a clear position in the *New Zealand Curriculum (NZC)* (Ministry of Education, 2007) as a multidisciplinary and integrated subject that is informed by disciplinary traditions and research within the social sciences. A conceptual focus drawn from the social sciences enables teachers to "think beyond the facts" (Erickson, 2002, p. 7) by filtering topics through a bigger idea about society and participation within it. This approach is particularly rich when contestable or problematic concepts are the focus for learning (Splitter & Sharp, 1995).

It is partly for this reason that topics are largely not prescribed by the curriculum,[1] with the exception of a handful of achievement objectives that expressly tie learning to New Zealand contexts such as the

---

1   It is also an artefact of the wider *NZC* (Ministry of Education, 2007) which emphasises school-based decision-making about curriculum content.

status of tangata whenua (Level 3), Polynesian and British migration (Level 4) and the Treaty of Waitangi (Level 5), and two that strongly infer knowledge about the *Universal Declaration of Human Rights* (Level 5, 6). Even this book has very few examples of specific social studies content knowledge. This is because learning that equips citizens to be critical and active cannot be pinned down to a fixed corpus of facts and information, but necessarily responds to contemporary social issues which arise in society.

One of the implications of a conceptual curriculum is that the process of context choice is more open and largely left up to teachers and teaching teams. How and why contexts are chosen is not often made explicit and there is little guidance given in the curriculum and in support documents about how to do this. The position underpinning the social studies curriculum, however, is much more explicit in Tikanga ā Iwi. In Chapter 2, Hēmi Dale outlines how Tikanga ā Iwi is underpinned by Māori values, knowledge and ways of being, central to which are Māori conceptions of active citizenship and indigeneity. The conceptual focus of this Māori-medium curriculum is intentionally emancipatory and Dale expresses that a key purpose is to enable greater expressions of Māori self-determination. Similarly, that Tikanga ā Iwi exists as a parallel curriculum is a salient reminder that citizenship education, and indeed, the notion of the 'ideal' citizen, cannot serve one model or prescription. Instead, we need flexible, open, and inclusive understandings of how citizenship is constituted, who belongs in our diverse nation, and how people can participate (Wood & Milligan, 2016). Citizenship is lived and experienced by young people and others in society in multiple ways. Therefore, educational frameworks which include, rather than exclude, such diverse expressions help to ensure that all members of society can participate equally and achieve recognition (Lister, 2007).

A concept-led approach, however, is not without its challenges and is the source of ongoing debate. The absence of prescribed topics makes social studies more problematic to assess (see Chapter 8), difficult to develop clearly articulated stages of progression (Ministry of Education, 2015), and renders social studies open to accusations of being "weak", lacking in substance, and prone to social engineering (Keown, 1998). At least two further challenges associated with this approach have also arisen. First, the absence of clear direction in terms of content knowledge opens up potential for novice and less experienced teachers to teach social studies badly, and can signal to some that social studies doesn't need experts as 'anyone can teach it'. This phenomenon explains why non-social science teachers are brought in to teach one class of social studies in numerous New Zealand secondary schools. Second, social studies is susceptible to stakeholder groups providing *de facto* content that takes advantage of teacher's freedom of choice. Over the years, social studies classrooms have been the dumping ground for a range of topics that encompass wide, varied, and at times bizarre socialising and political agendas. This has included sex education (as one of the authors experienced in two schools), careers education, life skills, character education, and the list goes on. Moreover, at the level of resourcing, a significant number of government and non-government organisations target social studies in order to meet their educational aims, often without a clear understanding of the nature and purposes of the subject. The existence of such challenges does little to diminish accusations that social studies teaching and learning is an 'inch deep and a mile wide' by failing to contribute to a cohesive body of learning (Partington, 1998).

However, there are a number of defensible, historically-tested reasons for retaining a concept-led curriculum. High levels of topic and content prescription risk teachers being less able to respond to the dynamic nature of society and contemporary social issues that are the focus of citizenship education. We do not suggest that social studies should focus solely on the present. Understanding contemporary issues requires a rigorous and in-depth knowledge of history (Wrenn, 1999, Whelan, 2006), and consideration of future implications and changes (Barr, 1998; Mutch, Hunter, Milligan, Openshaw, & Siteine, 2008). We *are* suggesting that teaching teams cannot review their learning programmes only every 5-10 years if they wish to make a worthwhile difference for students, and explains why some social studies teachers argue that textbooks are ill-equipped to keep pace with their more agile and responsive programmes (Taylor, 2011). This does not mean a continual and exhausting process of 'reinventing the wheel'. Instead, a conceptual approach enables the meaningful selection of contexts as vehicles for deep learning, including perennial and topical issues.

Moreover, centrally prescribed list of content knowledge tend to present a single position on a social issue, and work against learners' capacities to understand the range of values and perspectives involved, and independently make and evaluate alternative decisions and active responses that could be taken by themselves and others. As Abbiss argues in Chapter 1, social studies education contributes to disciplinary knowledge through an emphasis on understanding the contested nature of social issues (exploration of values and perspectives), how people adjudicate between different values and actions (engaging in social decision making), and the ways in which people can contribute to social change (through social action). A strong focus is therefore on the *processes of learning* through which social studies students develop knowledge, skills and dispositions that equip them to be citizens. Thus, while a conceptually-led approach ensures that social studies is not without substantive content, a great deal of the subject's rigour stems from an emphasis on its procedural dimensions. This brings us to the second question we address in this conclusion:

How do social studies students learn critical and active citizenship?

To answer this question, we need to consider the knowledge, skills, and dispositions that young citizens need now and in the future. For Hunter (Chapter 7), one response involves rethinking the literacies required for effective citizenship in a diverse and rapidly changing world. She argues that a multidimensional view of literacy more accurately maps onto students' lifeworlds and the capabilities they need to navigate societal complexity. In this view, social studies learning is in constant reflexive dialogue with the world, rather than being about a distant world. This links strongly to Barr's (1998) argument that citizenship education should focus on the *formation* of a defensible system of values, *habits* of reflection and critical analysis, decision-making *practices*, and real-world *experiences* of social and political action. Robust social studies learning is, therefore, as much about learning the processes of social inquiry as it is arriving at understandings about the social world.

If citizenship education is concerned with the real world practices of living and deciding how we will live together, it needs to be taught in a way that not only reflects the complexity of society and social issues but engages students in open, democratic dialogue (Hess, 2009; Holden, 2007; Milligan, 2007). This book has stressed the need for knowledge-able, skilful social studies teachers and learners who are committed to critical deliberation about issues and actions. In particular, a number of authors have highlighted the specific skills and processes of social inquiry that are of vital importance for citizenship education, and specifically what this means for a carefully planned focus on social issues (Chapter 3), exploring values and perspectives (Chapter 4) and taking social action (Chapter 5). Picking up on a point made in Chapter 3, social inquiry requires much more than formulaic implementation: "taught well, it is democratic citizenship *in practice* because it presents an entry point for students' own deliberations about critical, active and ethical participa-tion in society" (p. 58). This draws on what is relevant to young people's lives, supports their flourishing as human beings, and fosters the skills and dispositions of thoughtful, responsible, pluralist and non-violent cit-izens (Bermudez, 2014; Dewey, 1933).

Nevertheless, there is persistent evidence that the processes of exploring values and perspectives, making decisions, and taking action (Wood, 2013; Wood, Taylor, & Atkins, 2013) remain the 'hard bits' of social studies teaching and learning, even almost twenty years after Keown (1998) made this claim. In light of this, a number of authors have offered practical examples of how such approaches can be embed-ded within everyday social studies contexts, to richer ends. Taylor and Keown (Chapter 4), for example, offer pedagogies for paying closer attention to perspectives in order to better support students to navigate the contested, fluid, and colliding zones of different world views— "the very stuff of social studies learning" (p. 78). In Chapter 8, Rose Atkins and Peter Rawlins address some of the difficulties of assessment in social studies by proposing assessment strategies that shift away from a traditional focus on discrete content knowledge, and instead honour the contested nature of social issues and better reflect affective and participatory outcomes. Such shifts are important, for what we choose to assess ends up being what we teach.

Closely linked to critical and active forms of citizenship education is a commitment to a more socially just and environmentally sustainable world. For Aotearoa New Zealand, this involves a critical understand-ing of our colonial past, which has frequently served to exclude and minimise the citizenship rights of Māori and more recently other ethnic minorities (Godfrey, 2016). Returning to the contention that social studies learning must be in dialogue with learners' social worlds, one of the central aims of democratic citizenship education is to encourage young people to decide what should constitute social justice, and how they and others can work towards it. When founded on a Freirean (1973) understanding of praxis, citizenship learning that is linked to social justice involves a simultaneous process of action/reflection. In Chapter 5, Mutch, Perreau, Houliston and Tatebe suggest that a framework informed by critical theory, and which "honours diversity, challenges inequity, and promotes the actions, practices and processes of a fair and inclusive society" (p. 58) provides one way forward. They propose a process of teacher-led, student-led, and reflective inquiry as a pivotal part of a social action process. This reflective process enables a more transformative approach to social action that rests on an explicated commitment to social justice.

Towards social transformation

In the introduction to this book we argued for social studies education that is committed to *social transformation*. Like all educational agendas, a critical, transformative approach is not neutral. This does not mean that educators use social studies teaching to advocate for particular political parties or public policies. Instead, it demands that young people at school critically discuss and debate real issues affecting their lives and the lives of others, including the opportunity to use knowledge and understanding gained from classroom deliberation to critically participate in society.

Such goals also necessitate an inclusive, respectful, and supportive social studies classroom environment. It is impossible to support citizenship dispositions and action in students if classrooms are hierarchical and threatening to young people. A classroom climate which values the opinions of children and young people and provides space for their inclusion and decision-making is an important element of classrooms which develop strong citizens (Bishop & Berryman, 2006; Fielding, 2004; Schulz, Ainley, Fraillon, Kerr, & Losito, 2010). Classrooms which are taught in this way have been found to also enhance greater civic engagement both now and in the future. Such classrooms actively follow current events, discuss problems in communities and ways to respond, promote active dialogue and discuss controversial issues, expose students to civic role models, and study issues which matter to them (Hess, 2009; Kahne & Sporte, 2008; Schulz et al., 2010).

Acknowledging how emotions enhance and inhibit learning is an important aspect of a classroom climate which supports active citizenship through enhancing discussion and nurturing thinking. In Chapter 6, Tallon explores this, arguing that for too long, the affective dimensions of social studies learning (such as developing empathy and compassion) have been overlooked and understated. She suggests that the risk of overlooking these are that students may respond superficially to social studies contexts, may suffer emotionally by not 'performing' with the 'right' emotions or may feel excluded from the learning process: "a truly democratic classroom allows for a range of responses and treats each with sensitivity—respecting the dignity of the learner" (p. 114).

Within such classrooms, deep learning about society can occur. A rich, disciplined approach to understanding societal issues contributes to the moral wellbeing of our society and enhances the lives of students as communities. In relation to learning across the social sciences, Rob Gilbert (2013, 2014) is very clear on this point and we quote him at length here:

> Deep learning is an approach to knowledge rather than an advanced level of skills or understandings, and it can therefore be applied from the earliest year levels. The key requirements are that:
>
> - Students, under the guidance of the teachers, are engaged in asking and answering questions, which focus on why things happen, what should be done to solve problems, which arguments or solutions are most persuasive;
>
> - Concepts and skills are made explicit for understanding;
>
> - Learning is connected to real situations and events, to illustrate the complexity involved in understanding, answering questions and solving problems about the world;
>
> - Metacognition is a normal part of classroom discourse, in which teachers and students focus on the strategies used to address questions and conduct inquiry

- Various perspectives on questions, viewpoints and experiences are recognised, evaluated and incorporated into inquiries and proposed solutions;

- Answers and solutions are seen to be tentative, as there may be new information or further perspectives not yet taken into account. (Gilbert, 2014, p. 9).

Such approaches are strongly supported by the authors in this book, who retain an unequivocal commitment to deep and critical learning through social studies, and would add that opportunities for deep learning also arise from reflecting on authentic social action. Our hope is that this book offers social studies educators support, strategies, and inspiration to enact powerful social studies learning throughout Aotearoa New Zealand.

References

Barr, H. (1996). Citizenship education without a textbook: The example of New Zealand primary schools. Paper presented at the 76th *Conference of the National Council for the Social Studies* Washington, DC.

Barr, H. (1998). The nature of social studies. In P. Benson & R. Openshaw (Eds.), *New horizons for New Zealand social studies*. Palmerston North: ERDC Press.

Bermudez, A. (2014). Four tools for critical inquiry in history, socila studies, and civic education. *Revista de Estudios Sociales, 52*, 102-118. doi:/10.7440/res52.2015.07

Bishop, R., & Berryman, M. (2006). *Culture speaks: Cultural relationships and classroom learning*. Wellington: Huia Publishers.

Dewey, J. (1933). *How we Think*. Boston, MA: D.C. Heath and Company.

Erickson, H. L. (2002). *Concept-based curriculum and instruction: Teaching beyond the facts*. Thousand Oaks, CA: Corwin Press Inc.

Fielding, M. (2004). Transformative approaches to student voice: theoretical underpinnings, recalcitrant realities. *British Educational Research Journal, 30*(2), 295-311. doi:10.1080/0141192042000195236

Freire, P. (1973). *Pedagogy of the oppressed*. London: Penguin Books.

Gilbert, R. (2013). Social science education; Perrennial challenges, emerging issues and curriculum change. *New Zealand Journal of Educational Studies, 48*(2), 143–155.

Gilbert, R. (2014). Humanities and social sciences in the Australian curriculum. In R. Gilbert & B. Hoepper (Eds.), *Teaching humanities and social sciences: history, geography, economics and citizenship in the Australian curriculum* (5th Ed.). Melbourne, VIC: Cengage.

Godfrey, M. (Ed.) (2016). *The Interregnum*. Wellington: Bridget Williams Books.

Hess, D. (2009). *Controversy in the classroom: The democratic power of discussion*. London, UK: Routledge.

Holden, C. (2007). Controversy for beginners: How to keep calm and maintain control while teaching about controversial issues. *In Citized: Citizenship and Teacher Education*. Retrieved from http://www.citized. info/?strand=0&r_menu=res

Kahne, J., & Sporte, S. (2008). Developing Citizens: The Impact of Civic Learning Opportunities on Students' Commitment to Civic Participation. *American Educational Research Journal, 45*(3), 738–766. doi:10.3102/0002831208316951

Keown, P. (1998). Values and social action: Doing the hard bits. In P. Benson & R. Openshaw (Eds.), *New horizons for New Zealand social studies* (pp. 137–159). Palmerston North: ERDC Press.

Milligan, A. (2007). *Texting: a window into representing our learners' social worlds*. Paper presented at Philosophy Education Society of Australasia Annual Conference, Wellington, 6–9 December. Retrieved from https://pesa.org.au/images/papers/2007-papers/milligan2007.pdf

Ministry of Education. (2007). *The New Zealand curriculum*. Wellington: Learning Media.

Ministry of Education. (2008). *Building conceptual understandings in the social sciences: Approaches to social inquiry*. Wellington: Learning Media.

Ministry of Education. (2015). *National Monitoring Study of Student Achievement: Social Studies 2014—Overview* Retrieved from Dunedin: http://nmssa.otago.ac.nz/reports/2014/SStudies_Overview.pdf

Mutch, C., Hunter, P., Milligan, A., Openshaw, R., & Siteine, A. (2008). *Understanding the social sciences as a learning area: A position paper*. Wellington. Retrieved from http://nzcurriculum.tki.org.nz/Media/Files/ UV-files/Understanding-the-social-sciences-as-a-learning-area-A-position-paper-February-2008.

Partington, G. (1998). Social Studies in the New Zealand Curriculum. In P. Benson & R. Openshaw (Eds.), *New Horizons for New Zealand social studies*. Palmerston North: ERDC Press.

Schulz, W., Ainley, J., Fraillon, J., Kerr, D., & Losito, B. (2010). *ICCS 2009 International Report: Civic knowledge, attitudes, and engagement among lower-secondary students in 38 countries*. Amsterdam, The Netherlands: IEA.

Splitter, L., & Sharp, A. (1995). *Teaching for Better Thinking: The Classroom Community of Inquiry*. Hawthorn, Victoria: Australian Council for Educational Research.

Taylor, R. (2011). "Trickle-down effects: How developments in senior social studies shaped practice in junior secondary social studies." *Curriculum Matters, 7*, 195–212.

Whelan, M. (2006). Teaching history: A Constructivist Approach. In E. Wayne Ross (Ed.). *The social studies curriculum: Purposes, problems, and possibilities* (3rd Ed). Albany, NY: SUNY.

Wood, B. E. (2013). What is a social inquiry? Crafting questions that lead to deeper knowledge about society and citizenship participation. *set: Research Information for Teachers, 3*, 20–28.

Wood, B. E., Taylor, R., & Atkins, R. (2013). Fostering active citizenship in social studies: Teachers' perceptions and practices of social action. *New Zealand Journal of Educational Studies, 48*(2), 84–98.

Wrenn, A. (1999). Build it in, don't bolt it on: history's opportunity to support critical citizenship, *Teaching History,* 96, pp. 6–12

Author biographies

Jane Abbiss is a senior lecturer in the School of Teacher Education, University of Canterbury. Prior to moving into teacher education she was a secondary teacher and head of social sciences. She has an interest in curriculum issues, especially in relation to social sciences education, students' learning experiences and teacher education.

Rose Atkins is a lecturer in the Institute of Education at Massey University. Her research and teaching focus on assessment, effective pedagogy, social studies education and schooling in New Zealand. Rose has a particular interest in teachers' professional learning and assessment in social studies, and she is currently working with teachers to explore how assessment can be used to promote robust learning in social studies.

Hēmi Dale is a descendant of the Te Rarawa and Te Aupōuri tribes of the Far North of New Zealand. He is a senior lecturer and director of the immersion teacher training programme Te Huarahi Māori at the Faculty of Education and Social Work at The University of Auckland. He has been actively involved in the development of the Māori medium Tikanga ā Iwi learning area for the past 20 years. Other research interests include language acquisition and effective pedagogy in Māori medium classrooms.

Michael Harcourt is a social studies teacher at Wellington High School. He has taught for 11 years and has a special interest in social studies that is place-based and culturally responsive. In 2017 he is starting a PhD with Victoria University of Wellington's Faculty of Education.

Bronwyn Houliston is teacher in charge of history at McAuley High School in Otahuhu, Auckland. She is passionate about engaging her students in the social sciences. Bronwyn is currently a PhD candidate at the University of Auckland, investigating student understanding of history as constructed and contested.

Philippa (Pip) Hunter is a senior lecturer in history and social sciences education at the Faculty of Education, The University of Waikato. Philippa's research interests involve critical pedagogy in her teaching of history in initial teacher education, narrative research of problematised history pedagogy. Recent postgraduate teaching has focused on cross-disciplinary possibilities in secondary social sciences curriculum.

Paul Keown is an educational consultant and formerly a lecturer in education at the University of Waikato. His work focuses on social science and environmental education. Paul has a particular interest in values, perspectives, social action and communities of learning. His doctoral research was on social sciences teachers' professional learning using an online community of practice approach.

Hilary Kingston was a secondary social studies and history teacher. She has been a specialist classroom teacher and a head of department. Currently, she is a curriculum learning facilitator at University of Canterbury Education Plus.

Andrea Milligan is a senior lecturer at the Faculty of Education, Victoria University of Wellington. Her research relates a number of intersecting themes related to social sciences and citizenship education. This includes discourses of social and environmental justice, and the role of values, ethics and philosophy in education. Her recent research focuses on citizenship education in cultural institutions, and democratic education through local green environments.

Carol Mutch is head of school and associate professor in critical studies in education at the Faculty of Education, University of Auckland. She researches, writes and teaches about social studies, citizenship education, curriculum and research methods. Recently, following the Canterbury earthquakes, she has focused on the role of schools in disaster response and recovery.

Maria Perreau is currently a doctoral candidate in the School of Critical Studies in Education at the Faculty of Education and Social Work, the University of Auckland. She is interested in finding out how and why young people become social activists in New Zealand. Maria taught secondary English, social studies, history and drama in New Zealand and overseas schools prior to embarking on her journey in higher education.

Peter Rawlins is a senior lecturer and programme co-ordinator for postgraduate studies in the Institute of Education at Massey University. He teaches in the areas of assessment, mathematics education and mixed methods research. His research interests include assessment, educational policy, mathematics education and mixed-methods research.

Rachel Tallon is a former social studies teacher and resource writer. Her doctorate in development studies explored the intersection of the international development sector and education. She is interested in issues concerning empathy towards the distant Other, global citizenship and how young people work through the realities of social injustice. Currently she works as an education consultant and researcher.

Jennifer Tatebe is a lecturer in critical studies in education at the Faculty of Education, The University of Auckland. Her research and teaching broadly examine how socioeconomic inequality influences teaching and learning. Jennifer is currently involved in several research projects that explore how teachers understand wider school, social and political practices that reproduce inequities.

Mike Taylor is an initial teacher education lecturer at Victoria University of Wellington. Prior to this he was Head of Department for social studies (New Zealand) and Geography (United Kingdom) in secondary schools. His current teaching and research interests cross curriculum, pedagogy, and assessment and he is co-editor of the recent NZCER Press publication *Geography in Focus: Teaching and learning in issues-based classrooms.*

Bronwyn Wood is a senior lecturer at the Faculty of Education, Victoria University of Wellington. Her research interests lie at the intersection of sociology, geography and education and centre on issues relating to youth participation, citizenship and geographies of education. Her recent research focuses on young people's social action in schools, restorative practices in cities and education and global education policy.

Index

www.ingramcontent.com/pod-product-compliance
Lightning Source LLC
Chambersburg PA
CBHW080554270326
41929CB00019B/3304